HOW TO
BUY AND LET
A HOLIDAY
COTTAGE

HOW TO
BUY AND LET
A HOLIDAY
COTTAGE

Allison Lee

howtobooks

Published by How To Books Ltd
Spring Hill House, Spring Hill Road
Begbroke, Oxford OX5 1RX
Tel: (01865) 375794. Fax: (01865) 379162
email: info@howtobooks.co.uk
www.howtobooks.co.uk

British Library Cataloguing in Publication Data
A catalogue record for this book is available from the British
Library

ISBN 10: 1 84528 122 5
ISBN 13: 978 1 84528 122 9

Cover design by Baseline Arts Ltd, Oxford
Produced for How To Books by Deer Park Productions,
Tavistock
Typeset by Pantek Arts Ltd, Maidstone, Kent
Illustrations by Nicki Averill
Printed and bound by Bell & Bain Ltd, Glasgow

NOTE: The material contained in this book is set out in good
faith for general guidance and no liability can be accepted for
loss or expense incurred as a result of relying in particular
circumstances on statements made in this book. Laws and
regulations may be complex and liable to change, and readers
should check the currect position with the relevant
authorities before making personal arrangements.

CONTENTS

CONTENTS

PREFACE

Buying an investment home has been a dream come true for me. Make no mistake – it has been hard work and at times I have wondered if it has been worth the effort and financial outlay but, all things considered, I would recommend buying to let to any other ambitious person with money to invest.

It is important that you choose wisely; do your homework and find a sound property in the right location. Be prepared to put in some hard work preparing your property for letting and keeping up with the daily running of your investment. By taking your time and considering your options carefully, buying to let should provide you with an exciting opportunity and a viable financial asset.

This book can only be read as a guide because, of course, everyone's circumstances and financial position will be unique to them. Updates are made frequently with regard to tax and other financial aspects of owning and letting a property, and you should keep this in mind if you are intending to venture into the letting business.

Remember, you are in control of your letting business. Only *you* can decide if buying a property to let as a holiday home is a viable option for your own personal circumstances. There is no room for complacency in the property market and it is paramount that you seek professional advice relevant to your own personal circumstances.

Always remember, although property is often seen as a sound investment prices can – and sometimes do – go down as well as up!

Allison Lee

# ACKNOWLEDGEMENTS

I would like to thank everyone who has helped me in the writing and preparation of this book and in particular to Nikki Read and Giles Lewis at How To Books for giving me the opportunity of having it published.

Special thanks goes to Tony Briscoe at DHC Accounting who has advised me on the financial side of letting a property as a holiday home.

I would also like to thank John Hutchinson of Cendant VRG and Fiona Hamilton of Recommended Cottage Holidays for their assistance in helping me to understand the benefits of employing a letting agency.

Last but not least, I would like to thank my husband, Mark, for his endless patience. Without his help I would not have been able to realise my dream of owning an investment property and I would never have been able to write this book. Our holiday let property is an investment for our own sons, Sam and David, who made us realise the importance of creating a legacy – in our case through property investment. I hope our humble beginnings lead to a more profitable future for them.

CHAPTER 1 THE PROPERTY LADDER

Opportunities

There are many reasons why people look to invest in the property market. Whatever your own personal reasons for purchasing this book, it is probably true to say that you are exploring the possibility of buying and letting a holiday home with a view to making money from your venture.

In today's society when pensions are performing badly, people are working very long hours and everyday life is becoming a bind, it seems to me that many people are looking for an exciting opportunity that will give them pleasure and satisfaction in addition to earning an extra income.

The national state pension in Britain is unable to keep pace with inflation and, with the cost of living increasing, company pensions performing badly and poor job satisfaction, people are beginning to look elsewhere for an escape. The opportunity of investing in something that not only will give years of enjoyment, but also produce an additional income, is becoming more and more appealing.

Not so very long ago, the thought of owning a second home was virtually unheard of for a person of average means. Property developing had not gained the interest of the average household and house prices were extremely buoyant. Now, with property programmes dominating our television screens, a wide audience has been targeted and it seems we all have an opinion on the state of the property market!

Although it is possible to make good money from letting out a holiday home, I do not feel that this should be your only reason for investing. If the sole intention is to make money on a regular basis, then perhaps you should be thinking of purchasing a property with a view to renting it out on a long-term basis rather than as a holiday let. In my opinion, purchasing a holiday home should be as much for your own use as for the income it is likely to generate.

Will buying to let work for me?

A holiday home, if marketed correctly, should provide steady capital growth over time and, hopefully, the income generated from holiday lets should help the property to pay for itself. Certainly this should be your aim when looking to invest in the holiday let business.

Property is still a good investment. Despite the recent scares of plummeting house prices, it is always worth remembering that property prices rose by approximately 75 per cent in the 1990s despite a recession in the early years.

Before entering into the holiday let business it is wise to explore your other options, to ensure that you are making the right personal decision. Will you be able to make reasonable money from:

   a) savings plans;

   b) pension plans;

   c) unit trusts; or

   d) interest rates paid from the bank?

If you have been disappointed with the above, then perhaps it is time to turn your attention to buying property with a view to renting it out as a holiday let.

> **REMEMBER**
>
> *House prices can go down as well as up!*

So, will buying to let work for you? The answer to this question depends entirely on what you are expecting from your property and how much homework you are prepared to do in sourcing the right house and then preparing it for letting.

The right location

You will need to look for the right location. This must be an area that will appeal not just to you, but also to the average person looking to book a holiday. An important factor when deciding where to purchase your property will, of course, be the amount of funds available. Although this may seem obvious, it is all too easy for people to jump into buying property while being totally unprepared, and this can lead to disaster. In the main, do not let your heart rule your head. It is easy to fall in love with a property, and buying in this way may be fine if you are intending to make it your permanent residence. However, when buying a property to let, you must weigh up the pros and cons and look at the property as a business venture. The property must not be simply pretty and appealing to the eye – it must have the necessary potential to rent out and make your venture work!

> Take your time when selecting your property and don't let your heart rule your head. The property must be practical and work as a holiday let.

It will undoubtedly be easier for you to sell an area to holiday-makers if you yourself are passionate about it and know it well, but ask yourself why this particular area is so special to you. Is it simply because you have been visiting, out of habit, for the past twenty years or so and have never thought of going elsewhere or is it because of the area's outstanding natural beauty and fantastic beaches?

Ask yourself a few important questions before deciding on what kind of property to purchase and in which location:

1. Do you want your holiday property to be used mainly for yourself and your family and friends, with the opportunity of renting it out occasionally?

2. Do you want to rent your holiday home out most of the time?

3. Are you hoping that the property will increase in value?

4. Are you intending to market your property with an agent or will you try to let it yourself?

5. Is there a minimum return you would like to see with regard to rental?

The answers to these questions will make a difference to the type of property you buy and how you go about marketing it. If you are buying your property for the sole purpose of using it yourself and perhaps renting it to family and friends, then you will need to be equipped with much less information than if you are intending to rent the property out for much of the year to people you have never met.

Can I afford it?

Only you can answer this question accurately. It is absolutely paramount that you go into your business venture with your eyes wide open. Be aware of the problems and pitfalls you may encounter and always have a contingency fund for if things go wrong.

> Borrowing money has never been easier. However, it is vital that you are honest with yourself when deciding how much money you can *reasonably* afford to pay back. Strapping yourself at this stage is a bad idea, as the costs of furnishing and equipping your property can be high.

It is easy in today's society to borrow money. By simply picking up the telephone or going on line you can secure a loan. It is, however, vital that you consider very carefully the implications of owning a second property and the effect it can have on your finances. Although in reality the aim is to make the property self-financing, you will almost certainly make a loss in the first year and maybe even in the first few years, until your holiday let business becomes established. You will need to finance the decorating and furnishing of your property, not to mention covering the fees incurred in buying it and marketing it as a holiday home.

Your own personal finances must be able to withstand this loss initially if your holiday let business is to be a success. By failing to sort out your finances or overspending at the outset, you will be setting yourself up for a fall.

If you are in the enviable position of being able to finance your property purchase with cash, or you have been lucky enough to inherit a property, then the importance of examining your finances in detail will be reduced, as the main expense, repaying the mortgage, will not be an issue. Not having to worry about mortgage or loan repayments will, of course, ease the initial financial pressure.

If, however, you are intending to borrow money to finance your purchase, then you must be prepared to do your homework and look at the state of your finances truthfully. If you have never been good at saving, then bear this in mind when calculating how much you are asking to borrow. Banks and building societies will lend money depending on your earnings but is this really the best way of calculating how much you can afford to repay?

For example: two adults starting in the same job, on the same day, earning exactly the same amount of money will most definitely not be in the same financial position five years down the line. This is because no two adults or families are the same. People have different lifestyles and view their finances in very different ways. While one person may think they are affluent if left with £50.00 in their account at the end of every month, another may only be happy if they have £500.00 left over after paying all the bills. Others live constantly with an overdraft, often failing to make ends meet.

It is a good idea to make a list of all your monthly outgoings, including existing mortgage, loans, bills, insurances, etc., and then include how much you usually spend on socialising. Add to this a percentage to cover the cost of clothes and holidays and then look at how much surplus cash you have, after taking all your expenses from your monthly earnings. It is important to be honest with yourself at this stage and not kid yourself that you will be happy going without a holiday if you usually spend a month in the Caribbean every year! If you smoke and drink on a regular basis, the cost of this must be taken into account when calculating how much money you have to spend.

> You would be fooling yourself if you think that you can finance your holiday let business by changing your entire lifestyle in order to free up extra cash. Very often this does not work and you could end up with a heap of debts.

If you have a family who are dependent on you, then you must take them into consideration when calculating your worth.

When you have done your sums and taken *all* your monthly outgoings from your monthly income, you will be in a better position to see how much money you can actually *afford* to borrow rather than how much money you will be *allowed* to borrow. Armed with this information, you should be able to decide whether investing in a second property is a viable option for you and, if it is, find the right mortgage to suit you.

If you are left with £500 surplus cash at the end of every month, don't be tempted to accept a mortgage with repayments of £600, hoping that the income generated from the holiday let will cover the other £100. This is a recipe for disaster as you will have the stress of finding the extra income if the property is empty, not to mention having to pay the bills and finance the initial furnishing of the property.

In reality, the amount of spare cash you have each month will have to be used to:

1. Pay the interest on any mortgage or loan on the property.
2. Pay for decorating the property.
3. Pay for furnishing the property.
4. Pay for the upkeep of the property.
5. Pay any bills on the property, including gas, electricty, water, council tax, insurances, etc.

You will need to cover these costs from your existing income until such a time as your business venture is up and running. Remember also that, although you may make good money when you have guests in your property, the holiday season in different areas differs immensely, and there may be many months, perhaps over the entire winter period, when the property is empty. Despite not generating an income, you will still have to meet the mortgage repayments and keep up with the maintenance side of things.

Other financial considerations that you will have to take into account are:

1. Bank or building society setting-up fees. Depending on the type of mortgage or loan you opt for, lenders sometimes charge an administration fee or a set-up fee.
2. Legal fees in connection with purchasing your property.

3. Stamp duty.

4. Agent letting fees if you choose to market your property with an agency.

It is important to remember that while property prices haven risen dramatically in recent years, this trend cannot continue indefinitely and you must bear in mind that there is always an element of risk when buying property. You must ask yourself how much of a risk you are prepared to take and base your investment on this answer. It is probably not a good idea to buy an expensive property in a popular area if you are hoping to make a quick return. Resist paying over the odds for a property and bear in mind that an asking price is just that and may not be a true valuation of the property's worth.

In order to put things into perspective and reduce the uncertainty, it is a good idea to try to calculate how much you are likely to make from your investment once your business is up and running.

An easy method of calculating your profit would be to multiply the rental per booking with the number of bookings you hope to achieve, and then deduct any expenses. However, things may not be quite so straightforward if the amount you are asking in rent varies considerably from week to week and season to season. For example, you will be able to ask a much higher rental fee for a week in August than you will for a week in November. It is important that you do not command unrealistically high rents as this will almost certainly make your business suffer. A profitable approach – and this is what you should be aiming for – is to set your rents at a sensible level that will maximise your income by securing a high number of confirmed bookings throughout the year. This is of course much more preferable than securing just two or three weeks at a price which is out of the pocket of most holiday-makers.

When setting your rental fees, always be realistic and avoid the temptation to be greedy. A high number of confirmed bookings at a reasonable rate are preferable to one or two bookings at a premium rate.

Calculating yield

By spending a few minutes calculating the yield of your investment, you may get a better picture of how much you have profited by. There are several ways of calculating yield and the method you use will depend on whether you wish to calculate the gross yield or the net.

It is difficult to say what a realistic yield should be on a holiday let, simply because this will depend heavily on the area the property is in. The following examples show how to calculate the gross and net yields on a property worth £150,000.

Gross yield

Property value	£150,000
Annual rent	£10,000
Annual yield	**6.6%**

This amount is calculated by dividing the annual rent by the property value and then multiplying it by 100.

A more accurate percentage, however, will be the net yield, as this is the return after all your expenses have been deducted and is a much more realistic figure.

Net yield

Property value	£150,000
Annual rent	£10,000
Expenses	–£2,500
Profit	£7,500
Annual yield	**5%**

This amount is calculated by taking the total rent, less expenses, and dividing it by the property value and then multiplying it by 100.

In short, when calculating whether or not you can afford to invest in a holiday let venture, you must ensure that:

1. You are in it for the long term. You will not make a quick profit as your outgoings in the first year will almost certainly outweigh your profit, as you will have to prepare your house for rental.
2. You have a little capital behind you for emergencies.
3. Your existing income can cover the mortgage repayments of your holiday home when the property is empty.
4. Your existing income can cover the council tax, water rates and other bills when the property is empty.
5. You bear in mind that there will be ongoing expenses, for example a housekeeper, gardener, repairs and maintenance.

When you are happy with the state of your finances and are confident that you can meet the mortgage repayments and other expenses, then it is time for the dream to begin. Sourcing a property and preparing it for the holiday let market can be a very enjoyable and rewarding time, providing you keep a business head and take a sensible approach.

CHAPTER 2 LOCATION

Choosing the right area

When considering in which area to buy your holiday home, it is important to remember what will appeal to the average holiday-maker. However, if you have decided early on that your holiday cottage will be for the sole use of you and your family and friends, then obviously finding the right location may not be so important and you can simply purchase a property in a location that appeals to you.

If, however, you are intending to let your holiday home to other people, then it is vital that you do your homework and research the most suitable areas. A big factor in deciding which area to invest in will of course be down to finances. It is no good setting your sights on a beachside house in a busy tourist area if you have very limited funds.

> When deciding which location to invest in, ask yourself: Where do the people I know enjoy going on holiday?

When deciding on an area, think about the following:

1. Will the property be near to a beach?
2. Will the property be in a rural area or a city?
3. Will the property be close to pubs, restaurants and other entertainments?
4. Will the property appeal to young holiday-makers?
5. Will the property be more suited to the older generation?
6. Will the property have views?
7. Will the property be easily accessible?

When considering where to buy a holiday home, it is important to look at your own holiday history. Ask yourself which holidays you have enjoyed the most and why. Are there any places you would return to? Is there any place you would never visit again?

Facilities

Look for the attributes that will attract the kind of people you are hoping to aim your property at. For example:

1. Are you hoping to attract young families? If so, look for
   a) beaches.
   b) family-orientated entertainment such as fairgrounds and amusement arcades.
   c) swimming pools.
2. Are you hoping to attract older mature people? If so, look for
   a) good restaurants.
   b) nice shops.
   c) pleasant surroundings and scenery.
3. Are you hoping to attract young couples? If so, look for
   a) romantic settings.
   b) good restaurants and shops.
   c) nightlife.
4. Are you hoping to attract walkers and people who enjoy the outdoor life? If so, look for
   a) dramatic scenery.
   b) good walks.
   c) country pubs.

Just by considering some of the questions above it is easy to see why it is important to do your research prior to buying a property. You must know in your own mind what you are hoping to get out of the holiday home and who you are hoping it will appeal to. Although it is very important to actually like the property *yourself* in order to enjoy holidays there, it is equally important that you choose something that will appeal to most holiday-makers if you are intending to make an income out of letting it. It may be that your own dream holiday involves riding on steam trains or exploring old mine shafts, but it is probably fair to say that, although some people may be attracted to a property close to these kinds of attractions, others would probably avoid them like the plague. It is vital then that you find a happy medium. Perhaps try to find a property in a location near to a steam railway but not actually having one going through the back garden!

Obviously some areas will be more popular than others, and choosing the right location will depend heavily on how much money you have to spend. Areas such as the Cotswolds, Kent and Sussex can be very expensive for buying property, whereas the West Highlands of Scotland, Snowdonia and Northumberland are at the lower end of the scale.

Areas with good rental potential

Properties in different areas have different rental potential. Some areas have proved popular for many years with both visitors from this country and from overseas. It is probably safe to say that most properties in the following areas will benefit from a good rental potential:

Lake District	Kent
The Cotswolds	Sussex
North Yorkshire Moors National Park	Cornwall
Yorkshire Dales National Park	Devon
City of York	Hampshire

Shropshire	Isle of Wight
Suffolk	Snowdonia National Park
Norfolk	Anglesey
Wiltshire	The Cairngorms
Somerset	Scottish Highlands
Northumberland National Park	Scottish Locks (Loch Lomond, Loch Ness)
	Edinburgh

Holidays in these areas have always proved popular, but property can be very expensive. There are places, however, that may be within easy reach of the more popular villages but where the house prices are still reasonable. For example, if buying a property in Windermere in the Lake District is seriously beyond your budget, then try searching the surrounding areas. Often similar properties can be found several miles away from the main tourist area for a fraction of the cost. Nowadays most people drive and take their cars when holidaying in this country, so travelling a few miles to the main attractions will not be a problem. Another plus side of buying on the outskirts of a popular holiday town is that the area will almost certainly be a lot quieter and this is something that a lot of people prefer. Most holiday-makers are happy to travel a few miles for the action, if it then means a peaceful night's sleep away from the hustle and bustle of a noisy town centre.

> Consider buying a property on the outskirts of a popular town. Prices will be cheaper and the location quieter, while still being in easy reach of the main attractions.

It is probably safe to say that holiday destinations near to beaches or in beautiful countryside are a safe bet. These locations tend to appeal to most people, and therefore the potential to rent your holiday cottage out will be vastly increased. However, finding a dream property in an ideal location will come at a cost. Houses by the coast have, and always will, come at a premium. While at one time cottages in the countryside were abandoned for city life, good road and transport links have ensured that the country idyll in a remote spot is now much sought after and investors will pay a high price for this kind of property.

Distance to your property

Again it is important to do some research and source the market. Firstly decide which part of the country you are looking to invest in. Think carefully about what you are hoping to achieve with your holiday home. If it is going to be for your sole use and that of friends and family, then you will probably be safe looking further afield and a long drive to the property may not be to any detriment. However, if you are intending to rent the property out for holiday lets then the distance from your own home to your holiday property must be taken into consideration. The distance you travel will have an impact on things such as:

1. Visiting the property to ensure everything is running smoothly.
2. Routine maintenance to the property.
3. Problems and emergencies encountered.

If you live in Cornwall and choose a holiday property in Scotland, you have to ask yourself how practical this arrangement will be if things go wrong and you need to be at the property at short notice. A nine-hour drive is not an ideal scenario. This problem may be overcome if you are willing to employ people to manage the property for you such as a housekeeper, gardener and handyman, but of course paying all these wages will eat into the profit you make from your holiday rents.

Ideally you should be looking for a property within a two-hour drive of your own permanent home. A shorter drive would of course be more convenient, but if your holiday home is too near to your permanent residence you may not actually feel as though you are on holiday when visiting, or that you are far enough away from the everyday life you were hoping to escape!

If you have several locations in mind and are unsure of which to choose, then refrain from making a decision until you have sourced the property market. Look at houses for sale in all the areas you are interested in and see what you can purchase for your money before making a final decision.

Talk to estate agents in the areas you are keen on and ask them who the main people are that appear to invest in the area. Enquire whether they have sold many properties to investors looking to set up holiday lets.

Another good way of deciding on the location of a holiday home is to look at holiday brochures. Even if you are intending to market the property yourself, you would do well to look at the brochures offered by holiday companies to see what they are marketing, in which areas and for how much.

It may be that you have set your heart on a particular location, and by sifting through several holiday let brochures you will easily be able to see whether *your* ideal location is also considered the ideal location of holiday-makers. If your preferred area does not feature in the brochure, do not dismiss it altogether but give the holiday company a call and enquire why they do not have any properties in that location. In my experience, holiday companies are always on the lookout for new properties to let and are forthcoming with help and advice. It may be that they have had lots of enquiries from potential holiday-makers who would like to holiday in your chosen area, but to date no suitable properties have been made available. If, however, the holiday company advises you that the area you are interested in is not one that they would be looking to market a property in, it is important that you heed their advice. They have lots of experience in holiday letting and they know which areas are popular. If a holiday company refuses to market a property in a particular area, you can rest assured that this is because they know they cannot sell it as a holiday destination.

Deciding to pursue your preferred area will depend solely on what you want out of the property. If you want a regular income from a holiday let, do not buy a property in an area where other holiday properties are unpopular.

Sourcing suitable property

When you have decided on the area you would like to invest in, you must then locate a suitable property. At one time most people would only consider purchasing a house through a reputable estate agent. However, nowadays there are other successful ways of locating your dream property. Consider the following options:

1. **The internet**. This is fast becoming one of the most popular ways of tracking down a property. The internet is invaluable for people looking to invest in property in an area some distance from where they are living. The internet is a great way of conducting research and by going on line you will easily be able to get a feel for the types of property for sale in the area you are interested in and, most importantly, how much they are likely to sell for.

   Using a search engine will enable you to bring up property sites but I have found that sites such as www.rightmove.co.uk and www.ukpropertyshop.co.uk are the most comprehensive. These sites offer details of thousands of properties and by logging on you will be able to get a general feel for what is available in your chosen area.

2. **Estate agents**. These are still the most popular way of purchasing property. Do your homework and find out which estate agents are located in the area you are intending to purchase a property in. It is probably a good idea, initially, to call into the local offices when you are visiting your preferred location and introduce yourself to the staff. Explain what you are looking for and ask to be put on their mailing list. The agent will ask you several questions, such as:

   a) The type of property you are looking for, i.e. detached, semi, terrace, flat, etc.

   b) The number of reception rooms you require.

   c) The number of bedrooms you require.

   d) The state of the property you are looking to invest in, for example a property that requires updating or one that is ready to move straight into.

   e) The location you are looking for, i.e. town/village centre or outskirts.

   f) The amount of money you are looking to invest.

   Although it is important to let the agent know your maximum budget, I would advise all property hunters to have an open mind on the other criteria. You may initially think you can only afford a semi-detached or terraced house and state these as your preference, but if a detached property came on the market within your price range would you really turn it down? Tell the agent the minimum number of bedrooms you are looking for but also inform them that you are willing to keep your options open and will consider anything suitable that comes onto the market. Let's face it, it is the agent's job to inform you of the properties they have for sale and you only have to look at the details they provide you with to decide whether or not the property is worthy of a viewing.

Set your budget and stick to it! However, keep an open mind on other criteria. The fewer restrictions you set, the more properties you will have to choose from.

3. **Local newspapers**. These are another invaluable source of information and can be extremely useful for looking for properties with both agents and through private sales. It may also be worth considering putting your own advertisement in a local newspaper showing your interest in purchasing a property. Sometimes people who are considering selling their property may be tempted by a quick sale from someone already looking. A private sale is desirable for someone looking to sell as they will not have estate agency and advertising fees to pay.

4. **Word of mouth**. If you are a frequent visitor to your chosen area you will probably already have made friends there. It is worth mentioning in local shops and pubs that you are looking to invest in a property in the area and ask the locals to keep their ears open for you. Often locals, especially in small villages, know what is going on around them and 'village gossip' can be a good way of securing a property before it goes on the open market.

Choosing the right property

When you have found the area you wish to invest in, you will then be in the difficult position of finding the right property. The best advice I can probably give you at this stage is not to rush. Take your time and look at as many different properties as possible. Remember that you will be in the enviable position of not having anything to sell. You will probably either be financing your purchase with a mortgage, which should already have been secured, or as a cash purchase and this will put you in a strong position. Most sellers are keen to steer away from a chain and a quick sale is preferred.

Property criteria

It is a good idea to draw up a list of the things you would like your property to have. Perhaps make a list under three headings, *Essentials*, *Desirables* and *Things to Avoid*.

You may consider the following as **Essentials**:

1. Central heating.
2. Double glazing.
3. Outdoor area.
4. Good state of repair.

You may consider the following as **Desirables**:

1. Beach-front location.
2. Separate dining room.
3. Open fires.
4. Character features.
5. Garden.
6. Good views.

You may consider the following as **Things to Avoid**:

1. Property in need of renovation.
2. Roadside location.

3. Property very near to pubs, railway stations, etc. due to the noise factor.
4. Property in run-down areas.

Property to renovate

Your own list will of course be dependent on your personal preferences. Whereas a property in need of renovation may be one person's nightmare, if you are a builder or have contacts in the building trade, then this may be a very viable option for you to purchase a property at a cheaper price and do the work yourself.

Of course, considering buying a property that needs work doing on it will also depend on how quickly you are hoping to market it as a holiday let and how long you intend to be without rental income. If you decide on a house that effectively needs gutting and rebuilding, you may well have a project on your hands that will take in excess of 12 months to complete. While the property is not being rented out you will have no source of income from it, but it will be costing you in mortgage fees as well as the building work involved. Think carefully about the financial implications of this situation and how you will pay for the renovations. If, however, the house only requires a new kitchen or bathroom, or simply needs redecoration, this will probably only take a couple of months and then the house will be ready to market and therefore begin to generate an income.

Appealing to holiday-makers

The property you choose will have to appeal to a large number of holiday-makers, so it is important that you do not choose one that will alienate any prospective customers. For example, a picturesque cottage near to a fast-flowing river may look beautiful, but will it pose a danger to families with children and therefore encourage them to look for a more suitable destination? Likewise, a property with a railway line running at the bottom of the garden or near to busy roads could be equally off-putting. It is therefore important to take your time and choose your property carefully. Do not be tempted to try to save money by purchasing a property in a less desirable area or which has an unconventional layout as this could prove a false economy. You may struggle to get the customers, and even if you do get the bookings you are unlikely to get guests returning if they have been disappointed with the property or its location.

Generally, people who are looking for a holiday cottage are looking for something that at least matches the standard they are themselves currently used to, and quite often they desire something that bit more special. Holiday-makers looking to book a cottage are seeking the property that they themselves would like to own and therefore will expect your property to match their own criteria. Of course, it is impossible to please all the people all of the time, but you must strive to appeal to *most* of the people *most* of the time!

When deciding on the type of property to purchase, it is also a good idea to consider the practicalities regarding renting. Holiday lets are usually for between one and two weeks. This means that you are likely to have a high turnover of guests passing through your property. Your holiday cottage will need to be thoroughly cleaned in a short space of time and, although inglenook fireplaces and heavily beamed ceilings look nice, they can be a nightmare to clean, especially in a limited period of time.

What have I got to offer?

Before deciding on the location and type of property you intend to purchase, it is vital that you look at this question

and answer it honestly. We can all get carried awa
the dream and think that we will have the time and
to run a holiday let ourselves, but when the time comes
will this actually be a viable option? Will you really want to
travel to the property every week in the holiday season to
clean and maintain the property? Are you willing to be at
the beck and call of your guests? Can you make the time to
give help and advice when needed? Will you be available
to make your guests' holiday run smoothly? If you live on
the doorstep to your chosen property then the answer to
these questions will probably be yes. If, however, you have
a full-time demanding job and live a two-hour drive away
from the property, the answer to these questions will
almost certainly be very different. Even if you choose to
leave the running of your property in the hands of a housekeeper you will, from time to time, still come into contact
with your guests, not least if you are only checking that the
letting process is running smoothly. If you choose not to be
a 'hands-on' landlord and prefer to employ a caretaker, you
will still need to put time and effort into your business if it
is to be a success. How much time and effort you put in is
entirely up to you.

It is a good idea to do some preparation work in time for
the arrival of your first guests. Not only will this make the
job of the housekeeper easier, but it will also ensure that
the guests have ample information about the property and
the area they are holidaying in. The more information you
are able to furnish your guests with, the less chance there
will be of them pestering you! Guests feel happy if they
know the owner has gone to some degree of trouble to
make them feel welcome.

Take the time to source places of interest in the vicinity of
your holiday home and collect brochures and leaflets to
leave for your guests. If you yourself have had a particularly
good meal at a local pub, leave the details of the establish-
ment for your guests to consider. Likewise, if there is

somewhere you have dined out and had a really bad experience, mention this as well. Remember that the people holidaying in your house will only have a limited amount of time to explore the area. Most people are grateful if some of the legwork has been done for them and are happy to go with the owner's help and advice on the best places to visit.

CHAPTER 3
PREPARING YOUR PROPERTY

Appealing to the largest market

In order to make a good financial return on your holiday let property, you must always aim to appeal to the largest market. Once you have decided on your budget and settled on the area you would like your holiday home to be in, you need to ask yourself some important questions that will help you to identify how to appeal to the largest market. These questions are:

1. What do you consider the average holiday-maker to be looking for?
2. What would *you* expect from a holiday home *you* were renting?
3. Do you consider the area you have chosen to appeal mostly to families, young couples or the elderly?

Location is probably the most important factor you will need to consider as this, above all else, will determine whether or not your holiday home will be easy to market. It is all very well having a picture in your mind of a detached, thatched-roof cottage with roses around the door in a beautiful romantic setting; this type of property will almost certainly appeal to a large number of prospective holiday-makers. However, finding this kind of property and, more importantly, being able to afford to buy this type of property may prove a real problem. It is therefore essential to expand on your ideas and find a property that will appeal to as many people as possible, but also one that will not prove a headache to find and finance.

There are a large number of different properties to choose from, namely:

1. Detached properties.
2. Semi-detached properties.
3. Barn conversions.

4. Bungalows.
5. Terraced properties.
6. Flats and apartments.
7. Chalets.
8. Log cabins.

Each of the above will have some potential as a holiday let, but it is worth bearing in mind that some properties will be harder to market than others. Flats and apartments may appeal to holiday-makers seeking a base in city surroundings but may prove harder to let if they are in the wrong location.

When considering how to appeal to the largest market, you should also look at the ways you are able to market your property. You must decide whether trying to sell your holiday let yourself is a feasible option or whether you might be better suited to putting the property in the hands of an agent who will undoubtedly be able to reach a far larger audience. We will look at agents in more detail in Chapter 5.

Although location and property are the two main factors to consider when buying the ideal holiday home, it does not automatically mean that purchasing a rural idyll in a sought-after area will bring you maximum income. Once you have your holiday home, there are other factors that you must address in order to market your property and maximise your holiday let potential. More often, next to the location and the kind of property, the first thing would-be holiday-makers will enquire about is the price. They will be looking for a good-quality base in a great area, but at an affordable price. You must not undersell your property in order to keep it full, but neither must you be greedy. The average person has only a certain amount of money to spend on their annual holiday and, unless they choose to book a larger property and holiday with friends and family, and therefore split the cost of the rent, the price will have a huge impact on their booking decision.

Next to cost, another deciding factor will be the space and facilities on offer. Holiday-makers are usually looking for comfort and a bit of luxury. By ensuring your property has some of the points listed below, you will be on the way to achieving a high level of customer satisfaction and ultimately achieve a high level of bookings.

Facilities on offer

1. Cost of heating included in the weekly rental fee.
2. Good-quality, clean, modern kitchen.
3. Good-quality, clean, modern bathroom.
4. Additional toilet/bathroom.
5. Central heating.
6. Colour TV.
7. Games console together with a selection of games.
8. Good-quality, clean furnishings and fittings.
9. Secure car parking facilities.
10. Clean, comfortable beds.
11. Washing machine/tumble drier.
12. Outdoor furniture/barbecue.
13. Linen and towels included in the cost of the rent.
14. Clean, co-ordinating décor.

REMEMBER

Happy customers, who have enjoyed their holiday and considered the property clean and comfortable, are more likely to book another holiday with you. Keep the customer happy and they will return!

How should I decorate and furnish my property?

What would you expect to find in a property you had booked for yourself and your family? What things would cause you disappointment? The answer to these questions should help you to decide how to decorate and furnish your own property to ensure customer satisfaction. In the past I have holidayed in self-catering accommodation and, to be honest, I have been disappointed on several occasions with the state of the property that has greeted me on arrival. Some had not seen a lick of paint in 20 years, the furniture had seen better days and the properties had been generally run-down and tired.

Gone are the days when people can get away with renting out an old dilapidated cottage featuring 1970s décor and second-hand, worn furniture. In the age of computers when almost every household is able to view a potential holiday let on the internet, it is vital that your property comes up to the scrutiny of prospective customers. Would you personally be happy to pay a premium rate to stay in a property in a prime location if the interior failed to meet even the basic standards? I most certainly wouldn't and therefore neither would I expect my paying guests to settle for less than I myself would accept. It is probably fair to say that customers today expect, at the very least, the same quality of accommodation they find in their own homes, and quite often on holiday expect that bit more and perhaps even the added luxury. It is up to you to provide this.

> Furnish your property to the same standard you yourself would like to see in a property you were renting.

First impressions make all the difference. Truer words have rarely been spoken with regard to holiday properties. The first few minutes a holiday-maker spends in your property will determine whether their expectations have been met or not. A bad first impression could lead to further problems and confrontations, whereas a good first impression will set the seal for an enjoyable holiday.

Holidays are very important and yet can be fraught with difficulties. Your guests may have spent hours journeying to their destination, they may have been stuck in traffic, they may have had impatient children or animals to contend with, and they could very well be exhausted when they arrive at your property. They will have probably saved hard for their holiday and will almost certainly have been looking forward to its arrival. It is therefore your responsibility to ensure that they have not made a mistake by choosing to holiday in your property. That is not to say that you are responsible for your guests enjoying their holiday – that, of course, is up to them – but if you can ensure a warm welcome and an inviting, comfortable property you are well on the way to setting them up for a relaxing, enjoyable time.

When deciding how to decorate your property, it is important to remember that your house will take a lot of wear and tear. There will probably be a turnover of guests every week during the summer months. You may have little time to carry out maintenance on the property if it is heavily booked, and therefore it is important to furnish your property in an easy-to-maintain style.

How to decorate

Firstly, think about the type of property you have purchased. What works well in one type of property may be a huge mistake in another. It is best to avoid making the property appear bland, but using very bold colours to make a statement may only appeal to a small number of guests and alienate the rest.

Aim to add character to your property by using the rooms themselves as inspiration. For example, a country cottage with beamed ceilings and open fires will probably benefit from an 'olde worlde' kind of décor. Most holiday-makers booking a character cottage will expect to see 'chintzy floral' and it is therefore important not to disappoint. Be careful not to make the look appear dated and avoid going over the top. Mixing plain fabrics with floral ones helps to avoid overpowering a room and is therefore a good idea. If you plan to purchase a patterned suite, try to counteract this with a plain carpet and curtains and perhaps cream walls, so that the room doesn't feel claustrophobic with a riot of colour and patterns all fighting for attention.

Modern flats and apartments will probably be best suited to a streamlined look, and a minimalist design would appeal to most holiday-makers choosing this type of property.

Think about the practicalities of decorating a holiday home. Painting the walls in white or magnolia is probably the best option. The walls, particularly in high-traffic areas such as hallways and bathrooms, will take a lot of wear and tear. Plain emulsion is easy to touch up in a limited amount of time. Expensive wallpapers or specially matched paint colours will prove a huge headache when damaged. Neutral colours on the walls create a good backdrop for colours within the furnishings and they can also help to make a room seem bigger and brighter. Oppressive colours which draw a room in are best avoided.

When choosing the furnishings, opt for the best quality you can afford without being too luxurious. Good-quality furnishings may not be the cheapest on the market but they will stand the test of time and, in the long run, probably end up saving you money as they don't have to be replaced as often as cheaper furnishings. Penny pinching at this stage could well turn out to be a false economy. Suite covers, cushion covers, bedding, etc., will have to endure many washes and cheaper fabrics will quickly fade. Investing in good-quality items at this stage will ensure you will not need to change them continually as they become shabby.

Try to accessorise your property thoughtfully. It is easy to fill a house with knick-knacks and cheap trinkets but by doing this you risk cheapening your property by simply adding clutter. A few well-chosen ornaments will help the property feel homely without overdoing it. A couple of pictures hung on the walls will also help to create the homely feel you should be trying to create.

> When choosing ornaments and pictures to accessorise your property, remember the house will need to be thoroughly cleaned in a short space of time. Avoid clutter and make it easier to dust and keep clean!

Buying furniture and equipment

When deciding on the kind of furniture and equipment to buy to furnish your holiday property, always think in terms of quality. One of the most important elements of creating a positive impression for your holiday let is the quality of the accommodation on offer. You will never go wrong with good-quality furniture and equipment. Not only will they stand up to the test of time, they will enhance your holiday accommodation and please your guests.

There are certain safety regulations that apply to furniture and furnishings supplied in a holiday let property and it is vital that you comply with these. If you decide to market your property through an agent, they will have stringent checks in place to ensure that your property does not pose a danger to your guests. However, the onus on safety is down to you. We will look at safety measures in more detail later in this chapter.

When purchasing furniture and equipment for your holiday home, always bear in mind the number of guests you are advertising your property for. If for example your holiday cottage sleeps six people, it is unacceptable to buy a dining suite with four chairs, or insufficient plates, cutlery, etc. There must always be adequate seating in lounges and dining areas for the maximum number of occupants.

If you are advertising your property with an agent, they will have stringent guidelines for you to follow and will furnish you with a list of the minimum standard of equipment they expect you to provide in order to achieve a certain level of presentation. If, however, you decide to run your holiday let business yourself, you will have more freedom to pick and choose the furniture and furnishings you intend to supply. Marketing your property yourself does not mean you can skimp on quality furniture and furnishings. You should be aiming to please your guests sufficiently that they will want to return to your holiday home time and time again. This will mean an easier time for you with regard to letting the property and securing future bookings.

Try to decide early on what kind of look you are hoping to create for your property and keep your eyes open for the right furniture. End-of-season sales are always worth a look. You can often pick up good-quality furniture at bargain prices in the sales when companies sell off old stock to make way for new. The size of your property will be a deciding factor on the amount and type of furniture you buy. For example, a huge leather suite in a tiny cottage will be overpowering and impractical. A better option would be a comfortable cottage suite. Try to choose furniture with loose covers that can be removed for washing or better still, if your budget allows, leather furniture is a good choice as it can be wiped down and remains in good condition for many years.

Good-quality kitchen equipment is vital. The kitchen will have to stand up to a lot of wear and tear and, from my own experience, it is probably fair to say that holiday guests do not look after equipment in their accommodation to the same standard as they would their own. Who wants to spend their holiday scrubbing the oven or washing up?

With this in mind, go for the best-quality kitchen appliances you can afford. You will reap dividends in the long run. Opt for a self-cleaning oven to avoid spending hours trying to clean burnt offerings and grease from the insides.

A gas or electric hob with a minimum of four burners is essential. In a smaller property catering for a maximum of two or three guests you may get away with a hob providing three burners.

Invest in a dishwasher if you have the space. These are invaluable for giving crockery and cutlery another wash before your guests arrive, should it be necessary. If you do decide to provide a dishwasher in your accommodation, remember you will need to have an extra set of cutlery and crockery for each guest.

A good-quality fridge and, if possible, a freezer are also good investments. Although many holiday-makers will choose to eat out, it is always nice to have the option of dining at the property and, although a fridge and icebox are essential, a decent-sized freezer will be a welcome bonus to larger parties or families.

A microwave is probably considered a necessity by most people nowadays. They are inexpensive to buy and take up little space. Invest in a touch control pad rather than a dial as there is less chance of them being broken. Handles and knobs tend to take a lot of stick and the less equipment you have with dials the better. Microwaves can also be used as an acceptable alternative to a gas or electric hob ring.

Kettles and toasters are essential kitchen equipment and, as they are usually on display, opt for good-quality designs that compliment your kitchen.

Colour televisions must certainly be provided in a holiday property. If your house is in an area with very poor reception, try to remedy this with a booster aerial. In very remote areas where a broadcasting signal is impossible to gain, it is acceptable not to have a television; however, it is important that guests are made aware of this prior to booking. More and more people expect additional entertainment equipment and you may like to consider providing a video or DVD player. Properties catering for a larger number of people or families may benefit from the provision of a games console. Radios and music systems are also a nice touch and add to the overall luxury of the property.

Bedrooms must be comfortably furnished with adequate mattresses that conform to safety regulations. Each bed should have two pillows and it is a good idea to invest in mattress and pillow protectors to avoid staining and the need for constant replacement. Bedding should be adequate for the season and extra blankets should be provided for those who may need them. Good-quality sheets and pillowcases, which will stand regular hot washes, are essential. Sheets made from 100 per cent cotton are the best investment as these can be washed at high temperatures. I would recommend that you stick to all-white or pastel shades for bed linen as they do not fade like deeper colours and stay looking good for much longer. Colour can be added with bedspreads, throws and cushions.

Safety

As a landlord of a holiday let property there are certain safety standards that you will have to comply with. It does not matter if you are going to market your property with an agent or if you are going to market the property yourself – the same regulations apply. If you decide to put your property in the hands of an agent, they will furnish you with advice on safety measures and ensure that you have adhered to these prior to marketing your property. If, however, you decide to market your property on your own, you will have to make sure that you are aware of the current regulations and how to comply with them.

As a landlord you have legal obligations to your guests, whether your property is let privately or through an agent. If you fail to ensure that your property and its equipment are safe and you are found to be negligent in any way, then you are committing a criminal offence.

It is important that you keep up to date with current legislation as amendments are frequently made. An agent will be able to advise you of the current recommendations.

The age and type of property you have decided to purchase will affect the safety measures you will need to look at. Generally, new properties will comply with current safety standards, though it is always wise to get things checked if you have any doubts.

Older properties, though they appear charming and quaint, may pose a bigger threat with regard to safety issues. It is advisable to get wiring and appliances checked to ensure that they conform to current safety standards. If they do not, you will have to replace them before your property can be let.

The following is a check list for safety measures:

1. Gas.
2. Electricity.
3. Oil.
4. Fires.
5. Chimneys and flues.

6. Private water supplies.

7. Smoke detectors.

8. Staircases.

9. Balconies.

10. Upholstered furniture.

11. Glass doors and windows.

12. Child safety.

13. Gardens, outdoor areas and playground equipment.

14. Swimming pools.

15. Fire extinguishers and fire blankets.

We will now look at these points in detail.

1. **Gas**. It is important that you have all your gas appliances checked once a year. Gas appliances include boilers, fires, ovens, hobs and flues. You must ensure that any gas works and checks are carried out by a qualified CORGI gas engineer and that you are furnished with a certificate stating that your appliances are in good working order.

   - Never be tempted to fit gas appliances yourself or to save money by employing an unregistered fitter.
   - Ensure that your appliances are serviced annually.
   - Avoid buying second-hand appliances.
   - If you are in any doubt about whether or not an appliance is working correctly, have it checked.

   It is important to remember that people die each year from carbon monoxide poisoning, which can occur if:

   - Appliances are installed incorrectly.
   - Appliances have not been checked or serviced.
   - The chimney or flue is blocked.

- Appliances are not working correctly.

There are laws in place that require all landlords to:

- ✓ Ensure that all gas appliances are fitted and checked only by contractors registered with The Council for Registered Gas Installers (CORGI).
- ✓ Ensure that all appliances are kept in good working condition.
- ✓ Ensure that all appliances are serviced every 12 months.
- ✓ Keep a record of all safety checks carried out to show to guests or to be inspected by Environmental Health Officers as and when requested.

2. **Electricity**. Your main responsibility as a landlord is to ensure that the electricity supply to the property and the equipment available is safe. You are responsible for ensuring that the leads and plugs are correctly wired and fused.

   At the time of writing, there is no specific requirement for the regular routine testing of electrical appliances and wiring covering such objects as:

Washing machines	Televisions
Refrigerators	Hair dryers
Kettles	Electrical blankets
Irons	Lamps

   However, it is advisable to have all your major electrical appliances serviced annually as this is perhaps the only way you can be sure that you are complying with your duty as a landlord and ensuring the safety of your guests. By proving that you have carried out checks and taken all reasonable steps to ensure the safety of your guests, you will stand in good stead in the unfortunate event of an accident.

With regard to electrical safety, always:

✓ Ensure that any electrical work is carried out by a contractor who belongs either to the National Inspection Council for Electrical Installation Contracting (NICEIC) or the Electrical Contractors' Association.

✓ Aim to have the mains wiring to the property checked every five years.

✓ Ensure that all major electrical appliances are inspected annually.

✓ Check small appliances such as toasters and kettles at least every month.

✓ Keep a record of all safety checks to show to guests if requested.

✓ Replace broken electrical items immediately. Do not be tempted to buy second-hand equipment. Kettles and toasters are very reasonably priced and buying new will ensure peace of mind.

✓ Check flexes and cables for wear. If they show any signs of fraying, replace them immediately.

Any electrical equipment brought to your property by guests is not affected by the current regulations, as the safety of these appliances is out of the owner's control.

3. **Oil**. At the time of writing the regulations covering the installation and servicing of oil-fired appliances are less stringent than for those run by gas. However, it is important to remember that regulations can change at any time and are constantly being updated. To be safe, follow these guidelines:

✓ Avoid buying second-hand appliances – always buy new.

✓ Ensure your oil-fired appliance is inspected by a reputable qualified engineer annually.

✓ Ensure that the flue provides adequate ventilation for the particular fire or boiler you have. If in doubt, get it checked.

✓ Keep a record of any servicing you have had carried out on your appliance.

4. **Fires**. All fires used for heating can cause a hazard. Be particularly careful if your property has an open fire. Follow these guidelines:

    ✓ Provide a fireguard of appropriate size. The guard should be of a mesh design that will not allow fingers or other small objects to be pushed through.

    ✓ Ensure that the grate or fire chamber is in good repair.

    ✓ Provide a suitable container for storing coal and logs.

    ✓ Provide a suitable metal bucket or container for collecting hot ashes.

    ✓ Provide a good-quality companion set.

5. **Chimneys and flues**. Potentially lethal fumes can build up when chimneys and flues are blocked, and it is therefore paramount that airflow used to vent appliances is unrestricted at all times. When carrying out the annual inspection on your property, any reputable engineer will routinely check flues, but it is essentially your responsibility as the landlord to carry out routine maintenance and check chimneys and flues regularly.

Always:

- ✓ Ensure chimneys are swept regularly.
- ✓ Ensure flues and ventilation are checked annually.

6. **Private water supplies**. Many cottages in country locations are serviced by a private water supply. A private water supply includes water from springs, wells, boreholes and streams. As a landlord of a property with a private water supply you will be regulated by the Private Water Supplies Regulations 1991. The regulations are in place to ensure a reasonable measure of protection is taken towards consumers.

   Almost all private water supplies are tested by the local authority. The frequency of sampling will depend on the size of the supply and can range from less than once a year to in excess of 20 times a year. Sampling frequency is dependent on whether the water is used solely for domestic purposes or commercial purposes (this includes holiday lets), the amount of water being used from the supply or the number of people using the supply.

   If your property has a private water supply make sure you:

   - ✓ Talk to your local authority and inform them of your intention to let your property for the purpose of holiday accommodation.
   - ✓ Inform guests in advance, before they book their holiday, that your property is serviced by a private water supply.

7. **Smoke detectors**. It is essential that your holiday property is fitted with smoke detectors. They are inexpensive and the simple truth is that they save lives. There is absolutely no excuse for any landlord not to have smoke detectors fitted in their property.

If you market your property with an agent, they will insist on this basic requirement. The 1991 Smoke Detectors Act ensures the mandatory fitting of mains-powered smoke alarms in all new residential buildings.

Always:

✓ Ensure that you check smoke detectors and change the batteries regularly.

✓ Ensure that a minimum of one smoke detector is provided on every level of the property. Common sense should be used here as obviously the size of the property will also be a factor in deciding on how many smoke detectors to fit. A large bungalow with four bedrooms, although all the accommodation is on one level, will need to be fitted with several smoke detectors. If in doubt, install more detectors rather than fewer.

8. **Staircases**. These can be a potential hazard for children and the elderly. Follow these guidelines to avoid accidents:

✓ Ensure carpets are well fitted.

✓ If you intend to rent your property to families with young children, you must provide a secure stair gate for both the top and bottom of each flight of stairs in the property.

✓ Ensure that all stairways have a secure banister or handrail.

✓ If your property has an open-tread staircase, you must ensure that this conforms to current building regulations.

✓ Ensure that all staircases are adequately lit.

✓ If your property has steep, narrow, open-tread or winding staircase, you should mention this to any prospective guests, prior to them booking their holiday, in order that they can decide whether or not the property is suitable for their party.

9. **Balconies**. Although the idea of sitting on the balcony with a glass of wine appeals to most people, you must also bear in mind that a balcony should be seen as a potential hazard to guests holidaying with small children. If you have a balcony, ensure the following:

   ✓ The area is well maintained and in good condition.
   ✓ Adequate railings or walls are fitted around the balcony.
   ✓ That any railings or walls cannot be climbed on.
   ✓ Provide a key to the balcony so that guests with small children can restrict access.

10. **Upholstered furniture**. The Furniture and Furnishings (Fire) (Safety) Regulations 1988 set new fire-resistance standards for furniture. These standards apply to furniture supplied for properties intended to be let as holiday accommodation. Any furniture purchased after 1 March 1990 should already conform to these standards, as should second-hand furniture which has been bought after 1 March 1993.

    The regulations apply to upholstered furniture, including the following:

    Armchairs, sofas and dining chairs

    Beds and divans, including bases and headboards

    All mattresses

Sofa beds and futons

Cushions and pillows

Highchairs

Cots

Playpens

The regulations also apply to loose and stretch covers for furniture. Garden furniture which can be used indoors or out must also comply with these regulations.

Regulations do **NOT** apply to the following:

Sleeping bags	Curtains
Bed linen	Carpets
Duvets	Mattress covers

Any goods made before 1 January 1950 or the materials used to re-upholster or re-cover them are also exempt from the regulations.

Although it should, in theory, be impossible to purchase furniture today that does not conform to these regulations, it is always advisable to look for the relevant safety labels.

Although antique furniture has, in the past, been excluded from the regulations, it is advisable to check on the current position prior to renting your property out.

Further information regarding the Furniture and Furnishings (Fire) (Safety) Regulations is available from local Trading Standards Offices.

11. **Glass doors and windows**. The 1991 Building Regulations apply to internal and external glass doors and windows. These regulations have been in

force since 1992. The following rules must be followed:

✓ Any windows fitted to either internal or external walls that are 800 mm or less from the floor must be fitted with toughened glass.

✓ Stickers must be placed on glazed doors. These stickers must be at both adult and child eye levels.

✓ Safety glass must be fitted in any doors that feature glass panels 1500 mm or less from the floor.

12. **Child safety**. If you are intending to welcome families to your property, then it is essential that you ensure the safety of young children. Children are, by nature, inquisitive and they will want to explore their new surroundings. Cots, bunk beds and highchairs must conform to the appropriate British Safety Standards. When purchasing these items of equipment, always look for the signs that prove they are manufactured to the appropriate standards. Follow these guidelines:

✓ If you are providing a cot, ensure that the mattress completely fills the base of the cot and that there are no gaps between the mattress and the cot frame.

✓ Ensure that the width of the cot bars are appropriate and that an infant could not become trapped between them.

✓ Ensure that the cot is in a good, clean state of repair and that it has no loose parts or sharp fittings.

✓ If you are providing bunk beds, ensure that, where a base is more than 800 mm above floor level, there are no gaps in the base of more than 75 mm.

✓ It is acceptable to provide a travel cot in place of a conventional cot. These are often safer in terms of conforming to regulations, as they do not have bars or drop sides.

✓ Often, holiday-makers with young children and babies will bring their own travel cot. However, if you are marketing your property with families in mind, you should provide the basic equipment.

✓ Always ensure that cleaning equipment, matches, etc. are kept in a cupboard out of the reach of children.

13. **Gardens, outdoor areas and playground equipment**. Gardens described to holiday guests as 'enclosed' must be just that. Appropriate walls and fences must be in a good state of repair and all access gates must be fitted with a secure child-proof fastening. If your property is near to a potential hazard such as a railway line, stream or river, this information must be made available to any potential guests prior to them booking their holiday. If your property has a garden pond, ensure that guests are informed, again in advance, and tell them whether the pond is fenced or unfenced.

To ensure the safety of your guests, ensure the following points are followed:

✓ Potential hazards are kept to a minimum.

✓ All paths and external steps are well lit and in a good state of repair. If you intend to let your property in the winter months, ensure these areas are kept free from snow and ice.

✓ Any children's outdoor toys or playground equipment should be regularly checked and they must comply with the British Safety Standards

BS5696. All swings, climbing frames, etc. should be securely fastened to the ground.

14. **Swimming pools**. Although properties with swimming pools will undoubtedly be in great demand, as this is probably one of the most popular luxuries holiday-makers look for, you must also be aware of the potential dangers a pool could pose. In order to cover yourself in the event of an accident the following guidelines should be followed:

✓ Notices should be clearly displayed in the pool area stating the following important information:

1. Children must be supervised at all times by a responsible adult.
2. The pool area is NOT supervised when in use and that persons entering it do so at their own risk.
3. No running is permitted around the pool.
4. You are advised not to swim immediately after a meal.
5. No diving is permitted where the depth of the water is less than 5ft 6in (1.65m).
6. Emergency contact details showing local doctor and hospital telephone numbers.

✓ A lifebuoy and rescue pole should be provided at all times.
✓ The depth of the water at each end of the pool should be clearly marked.
✓ When not in use, the pool should be isolated. This can be done either by locking the doors to the pool area (if indoors) or having the pool area fenced off with lockable gates (if outdoors). Invest in a pool cover.

✓ The pool must be kept clean and have an adequate supply of fresh air and ventilation. Checks must be made either daily or weekly on the chlorine and pH levels to ensure the minimum standard required is maintained.

✓ Pool chemicals, pump and filtration plant must be kept locked.

Further information with regard to guidelines and regulations for swimming pools can be sought from your local Environmental Health Office.

15. **Fire extinguishers and fire blankets**. Up-to-date, reliable advice on the type of fire extinguishers to supply in your property can be sought by contacting your local fire brigade. Different types of extinguishers are recommended for different areas of the home. However, in principle the following points are worth bearing in mind:

✓ A minimum of one fire extinguisher should be installed in the property.

✓ A minimum of one fire blanket should be installed in the property.

✓ Fire blankets and extinguishers should be checked annually and a note of the date they were checked should be clearly labelled on these appliances.

✓ A notice informing guests of where to locate the fire extinguisher and fire blanket should be clearly displayed.

✓ A notice in the form of the following should be displayed in the property in a prominent position in view of all the guests.

IN THE EVENT OF A FIRE, FOLLOW THIS PROCEDURE:

1. Raise the alarm.

2. Ensure that everyone leaves the building.

3. Call the fire brigade.

4. If, and only if, it is safe to do so, tackle the fire.

DO NOT ATTEMPT TO PUT OUT THE FIRE IF IT IN ANY WAY ENDANGERS LIVES.

More detailed advice about the various regulations for the self-catering accommodation businesses can be obtained from Regional Tourist Board Business Advisory Services, the official organisations responsible for implementation.

The English Tourism Council also publish an excellent book on this subject entitled *The Pink Booklet*. This can be obtained by contacting them at Fulfilment Centre, Thames Tower, Black's Road, Hammersmith, London W6 9EL, or by telephoning 020 8846 9000.

A LOOK AT THE ROOMS ON OFFER

Available rooms

Before deciding how many people you are intending to market your property for, it is worth looking seriously at the rooms and amount of space you have available. Do not automatically assume that you will generate more income simply by marketing your property to cater for more people. There is no point in putting your property up for letting stating that it sleeps eight people if this means cramming extra beds into three standard-sized bedrooms. Although bunk beds enable you to accommodate more people in limited space, you will be alienating customers, as bunk beds can really only be marketed suitably towards children, and you are then effectively limiting your occupancy to school holidays.

> Do not be tempted to squeeze more people into your property than is reasonably acceptable. Your guests will feel cramped and suffer from the lack of privacy, making it unlikely for them to want to return.

When deciding on the number of people you intend to accommodate, in addition to the number of bedrooms you have on offer, look at the size of your living accommodation. You will need to have an armchair or comfortable sofa seating for every guest you aim to accommodate, and your lounge must therefore have adequate space. Your kitchen and dining area must also be looked at carefully. Is your kitchen really large enough to cater for ten adults or would you be better aiming for eight or even six? There should be adequate seating in your dining area to enable every guest to sit comfortably at the same time.

Another point worth considering is the number of bathrooms your property has to offer. If you market your holiday let through an agent, they may well insist on a certain number of bathrooms if you are intending to let your property to a large number of guests. It is far from ideal to market a property for ten guests if they all have to queue for one bathroom. It is usually expected that a property large enough to accommodate six people or more should have a second toilet and hand basin.

Finally, take into account your outdoor area. If you have a garden or patio suitable for entertaining, think about providing a barbecue for your guests to use. If you do decide to make the most of your outdoor area, make sure you have sufficient garden furniture to accommodate all of your guests together.

What to provide in each room

Before deciding what to provide in each room of your property, it is a good idea to sit down and work out how much money you can reasonably afford to spend. It is probably true to say that your initial outlay will be rather high, as you will have the whole house to furnish. Look at the amount of rent you are intending to charge and work out how many weeks' rental you will need to receive to recoup the money spent on furnishing the property. Depending on the area and type of property you have, you may only be able to let your holiday home during the summer season, say for 12–16 weeks per year, and in this case it will obviously take you much longer to recoup your costs than if you have the potential to let your property for 30 or more weeks per year. Like any new business venture, you will need to invest money from the start in order to set up your business and before you can begin to reap the profits. There are three options you can choose from when deciding how much to spend on furnishing your property.

1. **Expensive**. This includes top-of-the-range furniture, sumptuous furnishings, hand-made kitchens, whirlpool baths, etc. The type of property you own will have to be impressive enough to justify this kind of expense, and the rent you are able to command will have to be sufficient to recoup your costs.

2. **Middle of the road**. This is probably the best option, and is the one that most landlords opt for. Choose reputable suppliers and try to do your shopping when the sales are on. It is possible to purchase bed linen, kitchen accessories, towels, cushions, etc. at knockdown prices in stores such as Next, Marks & Spencer and Laura Ashley. You can create a statement with luxurious fabrics at a fraction of the cost if you shop carefully and have an eye for a bargain.

3. **Cheap**. This option is probably a false economy, although in some cases it may be a necessity. If you do choose to purchase cheap goods from discount stores, be prepared to have to replace items more frequently as they will not stand up to the wear and tear of letting. If your funds are very limited then perhaps look at saving money on items such as crockery and glasses, towels and bedding initially, and use the bulk of your capital to purchase larger items such as decent beds, lounge furniture and a dining suite. These items will be expensive to replace frequently, whereas soft furnishings can often be replaced cheaply as and when necessary. Remember also that if you choose to furnish your property at budget prices, it will be apparent to your guests, and therefore you will be unable to charge too high a rental fee. Always remember that guests expect the price they pay to reflect the quality of the accommodation they get.

You will be unable to get away from the expense of the large items needed to furnish your property and you may be restricted in how much money you can save. Beds, lounge suites, tables and chairs, flooring, etc. will all need to be budgeted for. The next part of this chapter will look at each of the rooms separately and examine the essentials that it will be necessary for you to provide.

> The way you choose to furnish your property will be reflected in the rental charges you can command. Budget furnishings can only be used in the lower rental market. Look for good-quality furniture and furnishings to reflect your property's true rental potential.

Kitchen

It is highly unlikely that you will replace the entire kitchen in your newly acquired property unless it is very dated and shabby. Often a kitchen can be updated quite easily by simply replacing the cupboard doors and handles. If, however, you have to replace the entire kitchen, go for the best-quality units you can afford. The kitchen is a high-traffic area and will be prone to huge amounts of wear and tear. Cheap units will become worn and damaged very quickly and the expense of refurbishing the entire kitchen is not something you should want to be doing every couple of years. Opt for easy-to-clean cupboard doors, and avoid patterned grooves or bevelled edgings which attract dirt and grease and can be difficult to clean in a short space of time.

Work surfaces should be clean and in good condition, free of cracks and splits, which harbour dirt, germs and food particles. A window or other adequate ventilation is paramount in the kitchen. Good-quality flooring is also essential. Opt for a wipe-clean floor of either linoleum or tiles and avoid any type of carpet that will be difficult to clean if spills are made. Rugs can be dangerous on tiled floors or linoleum, and these should be avoided at all costs in the kitchen area.

Appliances

After the actual units, white goods and electrical items will be your biggest expense in the kitchen. You will need to provide a good-quality, clean **fridge and freezer** (these can be combined). If space is limited, it is acceptable to provide a fridge with a small freezer compartment, though this may alienate larger parties of guests and families who will see a full freezer as a necessity. If you have the space, it is best to provide both. Another expense is the **oven and hob**. If your kitchen does not have a built-in oven, try to purchase one that is self-cleaning. These do cost more but they will save you a great deal of time when cleaning your property. There is nothing worse for new guests than to be greeted by a filthy oven: cleaning the oven is not something that is high on the holiday-maker's agenda. In the few hours you or your housekeeper has to clean your property, after guests leave and before the new arrivals, you do not want to be faced with scrubbing the oven. Choose your hob carefully: again, look at the cleaning aspect and opt for something that is easy to wipe over.

Washing machines are considered a necessity in any holiday home. It *is* true to say that some guests would not dream of washing on holiday, especially if they are only at the property for a week. However, on the other hand guests with young children may need to wash frequently. Opt for a washing machine with a high spin speed and a half wash or economy option.

Although you may not consider a **tumble dryer** to be a necessity for holiday-makers, you may like to think about how your guests will dry their washing if the weather is poor. If you are going to provide a tumble dryer I would advise you to purchase one separate from your washing machine. Combined washer-dryers are often more expensive to run. If you opt for a high spin speed on your washing machine, the time that clothes will take to dry in a tumble dryer will of course be drastically reduced and it will therefore be more economical.

It can be a difficult decision to make regarding the provision of a dishwasher. Although considered a luxury not many years ago, they are now probably classed as a necessity in most households. Certainly properties that accommodate parties of six guests or more would benefit from having one.

Microwaves are another essential piece of kitchen equipment. Touch pad controls are much simpler to use and avoid the wear and tear of constantly used dials.

A **vacuum cleaner** is an essential piece of household equipment. Although holiday-makers are unlikely to spring-clean your home, they probably will run around with a vacuum cleaner from time to time, especially if they have pets or young children. Choose a good-quality cleaner that does not require dust bags. Guests may use the cleaner but they will be loathe to empty a full dust bag and therefore the vacuum cleaner will not work to its full capacity. Combined wet and dry vacuum cleaners are a good investment, as minor spills can be cleaned up easily, but these can be expensive. If your property is on several levels consider investing in two vacuum cleaners so that guests and you/your housekeeper do not have to carry heavy equipment up several flights of stairs. If you are intending to provide more than one vacuum cleaner, opt for an upright and a cylinder type and please everyone!

REMEMBER

If you can afford it and your property has sufficient space to accommodate it – then buy it!

You can never have too many gadgets in the kitchen and holiday-makers love to be impressed. If there is a lot of competition near you for holiday lets, then make sure your property has advantages over the others which will make guests want to book yours!

Kitchen equipment

Equipping the kitchen will probably take up a large amount of your budget, as there are many essential items to provide. It is difficult to know exactly what to provide in a holiday let, but don't assume that most holiday-makers eat out every day and therefore you only need to provide the very basic items. Try to anticipate every holiday-maker's requirements and aim to please as many guests as possible with a variety of good-quality kitchen accessories. It is not easy to please everyone and what one person may consider a luxury another may consider an absolute necessity. It is vital that you provide a minimum of one set of cutlery and crockery for every guest your property can accommodate, and more if your property has a dishwasher. Take into account the possibility of breakages and ensure that there are at least a couple of extra cups, glasses, plates, etc. for this eventuality.

If you decide to market your property with an agency, they will be able to furnish you with details of what they consider to be the minimum requirements for a property of your size. However, if you are intending to market the property yourself, the following is a guide to the *minimum* amount of equipment you will need to provide in your kitchen.

Items per person (extra sets will be needed if your property has a dishwasher)

Cereal bowl	Dessert spoon
Soup bowl	Teaspoon
Dessert bowl	Soup spoon
Dinner plate	Egg cup
Side plate	Tumbler
Mug	Wine glass
Teacup and saucer	Beer glass
Table fork and dessert fork	Spirit glass
Table knife and side/butter knife	

Remember that provision of the above items must also take into account any breakages and you are advised to make sure you have spares.

Kitchen equipment

Bread board

Chopping boards (plastic – clearly labelled for meat, vegetables, etc.)

Biscuit/cake tins

Storage containers, for example Tupperware

Butter dish with a lid

Toaster

Toast rack

Teapot

Kettle (preferably electric)

Coffee maker/cafetiere/cappuccino maker

Tray (preferably two)

Water jug

Serving dishes

Milk jug

Tea, coffee and sugar canisters

Sugar bowl

Grater

Ice tray

Iron

Ironing board

Measuring jug

Colander

Condiment set

Kitchen scales

Salad bowl and salad servers

Flower vases

Fruit bowl

Gravy boat

Oven wear
A minimum of one large, one medium and one small saucepan with lids (if your property accommodates a large number of guests, make extra provisions).

Baking tray or tin

Casserole dish with a lid

Frying pan

Roasting dish

Pie dish

Yorkshire pudding tins

Kitchen utensils

Knives – a good selection of quality knives, including a carving knife, a vegetable knife and a bread knife.

Knife sharpener	Serving spoons (amount dependent on number of guests)
Bottle opener/corkscrew	
Scissors	Ladle
Potato peeler	Fish slice/spatula
Potato masher	Straining spoon
Tin opener	Trivets
Sieve	Tablespoons
Wooden spoons	Tea strainer
Whisk	Mixing bowls

Kitchen sundries

Tea towels	Duster
Oven glove	Vacuum cleaner
Apron	Clothes line
Tablecloths	Clothes pegs
Table mats	Clothes prop (if necessary)
Coasters	Torch
Dishcloths	Spare light bulbs and batteries
Floorcloth	Doormat
Mop	Washing-up bowl
Bucket	Drainer
Sweeping brush	Dustbin with lid
Dustpan and brush	

A selection of cleaning equipment (it is a good idea to provide the basics such as toilet cleaner, washing-up liquid, dishwasher tablets, disinfectant and a bathroom/kitchen cleaner – not every guest will use them but they are more likely to do *some* cleaning if the equipment is provided. Guests are unlikely to want to pay for materials to clean *your* house).

Useful additions

If you allow pets in your property, then provide a mat and two feeding bowls.

If you allow smoking in your property, provide ashtrays. In addition to the above items that many people would consider essential, you may also wish to add other pieces of equipment, perhaps objects that you yourself would use. For example, useful items not considered essential but that are often useful and would be appreciated, are:

Garlic press	Bottle stoppers
Pestle and mortar	Steamer
Ice-cream scoop	Nutcrackers
Blender	Lemon zester
Wine rack	

Providing a selection of cookery books would add a nice personal touch and you will be surprised at how many people will use them. Often people who enjoy cooking but who lack the time at home will indulge their passion on holiday, and trying new recipes is something they will enjoy.

It is *essential* that your kitchen is equipped with the basic safety provisions such as:

Fire extinguisher	Fire blanket

These items should be placed in full view and be clearly labelled.

Living room

This is another room which, initially, will be rather expensive to furnish. Although you do not need to buy everything top of the range, you must ensure that the living areas of your property are comfortable and spacious enough to accommodate the maximum number of guests it is advertised for.

When deciding on the type of furniture to purchase, look carefully at the proportions of the room and buy appropriately. Remember, if your property accommodates six people then there must be sufficient seating from either armchairs or sofas to house everyone. Leather suites, though initially expensive to purchase, will last for years. They are hard-wearing and easy to clean. Often a damp cloth is all that is needed to clean up spills and remove marks. Fabric upholstery will get dirty quickly, and unless you choose furniture with removable covers it will be difficult to keep this kind of suite looking good, especially if you are allowing young children and dogs to use your property. If you do purchase an upholstered suite, opt for good quality and consider having a stain guard added to ensure the furniture stays looking good for as long as possible.

Next to the suite the other expense you will have when furnishing the lounge area is the flooring. If your property is already carpeted to a decent standard, try to work with what you have. New carpets, although they will enhance your property, are not a good idea in a holiday let unless you have no other option, as they will get dirty. Guests will invariably walk through your house in their outdoor shoes, treading mud, sand, etc. into the flooring. Dogs may have muddy paws, children will spill drinks and food will get dropped. New carpets will only stay looking new for a relatively short time. If the existing carpet is in good condition, consider having it professionally cleaned and purchase furniture and accessories that will blend with it. A reputable carpet-cleaning company will clean the carpets in an average-sized three-bedroom house for around £300. Shop around and ask if they will offer a discount to you as a holiday home owner, if you agree to have your carpets cleaned by the same company annually. Depending on whether or not you are allowing pets and children into your property and on how many weeks you are intending to let your holiday home per year will be the deciding factor when planning how often your carpets will need to be professionally cleaned. It is probably fair to say that a good, thorough clean once every 12–18 months will be necessary. This may seem an expense but carpets harbour dirt and dust mites no matter how often you vacuum, and it is much more economical to have them cleaned regularly than to replace them.

Another option you may like to consider for flooring is bare floorboards. This will obviously depend on the age of your property and the condition of the floorboards. Bare boards are hard-wearing and mud and spills are much easier to get up from them than from carpets; however, you should take into account the noise factor and the need for sanding and re-sealing.

Entertainment equipment such as a colour television is a necessity in a holiday home. Ensure that the reception is good and provide a booster aerial if necessary.

Invest in good-quality, medium-weight lined curtains. If you purchase cheap curtains your guests will be able to tell and you will risk cheapening the rest of the room. Good-quality curtains do not have to be made to measure and they can be purchased at reasonable prices in the sales of shops such as Marks & Spencer, Next and Laura Ashley. Spending a little extra on curtains will pay off as they will last years and enhance the look of your living room.

In addition to the larger items required to furnish your property's living room, the following is a list of items considered essential by today's holiday guests:

Video recorder or DVD player

Occasional tables

Table lamps

Cushions and throws

Fire accessories such as a fire-guard, coal bucket, log basket and companion set

Pictures or wall hangings

Ornaments

In addition to the above 'essentials', consider providing some or all of the following to help your guests feel comfortable and enjoy their holiday:

Games console and games

Videos or DVDs

Games – classic family games such as Monopoly, Ludo, etc. are a safe bet

Jigsaws

Playing cards

Leaflets for places of interest

Local maps

Visitor's book

CD player and a selection of CDs

Wastepaper bin

Pictures

Dining room/area

If your dining area is an extension of either the living room or kitchen, try to continue the same theme throughout. For example, if your dining area leads from the lounge and has two windows, choose the same curtains and upholstery for the chairs/suite to 'tie' the room together and create a feeling of continuity.

A good-quality dining suite is essential. It is important to remember that all your guests must be able to be seated comfortably around the dining table together. Think carefully about the kind of dining room chairs you choose. Fabric-covered chairs may get marked with food and drink and plain wooden chairs risk being uncomfortable. A good idea, therefore, would be either to select chairs with removable covers that can be machine washed or provide cushions for additional comfort to wooden seating.

Flooring is another difficult choice. If your dining area is an extension of the lounge, then the choice will already be made for you as it is likely to be carpeted the same. If, however, you have a separate dining room or your dining area leads from the kitchen, then consider either a laminate floor, bare boards, linoleum or tiles. These types of floors are easy to keep clean and food spills can be wiped up with ease.

Others items you should provide in the dining room/area are:

✓ Lamp

✓ Wastepaper basket

✓ Highchair (if your property accommodates babies or young children)

✓ Pictures or wall hangings

✓ Ornaments

In addition to the above necessities, you may like to provide an extra touch with a display cabinet or wine rack.

Bedrooms

The most expensive items of furniture you will need to purchase for the bedrooms will be the beds. It is important that you do not buy very cheap mattresses as these will be uncomfortable and need replacing often. A good-quality mattress should last several years, depending on how often your property is let and therefore how often the beds are slept in.

Try to accommodate the majority of guests by opting for medium, interior-sprung mattresses. Slatted bases are easy for cleaning, as most vacuum attachments can reach underneath. On the other hand, drawer divans can be very useful for storage.

It goes without saying that there must be sufficient beds for the number of guests your property can accommodate and, if you supply bunk beds, your guests must be made aware of this before they book their holiday. Bunk beds can really only be successfully marketed for children and by providing these, although you may be able to sleep an extra person, you will be limiting your holiday lets to families and therefore primarily to the school holidays. Limitations like these should be avoided whenever possible.

If your property does not have fitted furniture, you must provide somewhere to hang and store guests' clothes.

Bedroom carpets need not be expensive as very little of them will actually be on display once the furniture is in place. Good-quality lined curtains or blinds should be hung at the windows. Consider the privacy aspect of your bedrooms and, if necessary, provide net curtains or voiles if your property is overlooked.

Other items you will have to provide in the bedrooms are:

- ✓ Bed linen – a minimum of two complete sets of bed linen should be purchased for each bed. It may be preferable to provide three sets if laundering is a problem.
- ✓ Washable mattress protectors for each bed. It is a good idea to provide a plastic waterproof cover if you are letting your property to families with young children.
- ✓ Pillows – two for each guest
- ✓ Duvets – one per bed
- ✓ Pillow protectors
- ✓ Additional blankets
- ✓ Wardrobes – these may be fitted or freestanding
- ✓ Chest of drawers or dressing table
- ✓ Mirror
- ✓ Bedside tables

✓ Bedside lamps

✓ Coat hangers

✓ Pictures

You can furnish your bedrooms to a good standard in a way that will appeal to your guests by spending a little more money on extras. Items such as a bedside clock and radio and a hair dryer will make all the difference. Small ornaments should be used to dress the room.

Bathrooms

If the bathroom suite is in good condition then this room should be relatively inexpensive to furnish. If you are thinking of replacing the suite, opt for one in white with quality fittings that won't date.

✓ Bathroom cabinet

✓ Mirror

✓ Towel rail

✓ Toilet brush and holder

✓ Toilet roll holder

✓ Soap dish

✓ Tumblers

✓ Waste paper bin with a lid

✓ Bath mats

✓ Towels (one hand towel and one bath towel per person)

You will need to provide the following in the bathroom: Additional items to add that luxury feel could be bathroom scales, toiletries and a shaving adapter plug. Toiletries can be bought in bulk, which makes them cheaper to purchase. Rotalux Ltd sells a good range of exclusive toiletries at very reasonable prices. For a brochure and further information, contact Rotalux Ltd on 01704 500386 or visit their website: www.hoteltoiletries.com

Ideally the flooring in the bathroom should be washable, for example linoleum or tiles, and bath/pedestal mats provided.

Conservatory

If you are lucky enough to have a conservatory at your property, make sure you furnish it in a manner that will enable it to be used all year round. If there is no heating then consider adding some in order that guests can utilise this area throughout the winter months. A tiled floor is a good choice in a conservatory as guests will probably be entering this space from the garden/outdoor area.

Consider furnishing the conservatory with the following items:

✓ Cane or wicker furniture with adequate seats to accommodate the number of guests
✓ Coffee table
✓ Lamp

Personal touches such as a wine rack and ornaments will add a homely feel.

Laundry room

Your property may or may not have a separate utility room, but even if it doesn't you will have to provide the following items, which should be stored in an appropriate area:

✓ Iron
✓ Ironing board
✓ Laundry baskets (one for clean clothes and one for dirty laundry)
✓ Clothes line
✓ Pegs
✓ Clothes prop
✓ Clothes airer

You may also decide to provide soap powder and fabric conditioner, but this is often a personal choice and will also depend on the rental fees you are charging.

Garden and outdoor area

If your property has a garden or small patio area, it is a good idea to provide garden furniture for your guests. Even the smallest outdoor area can be enjoyed in the summer months and guests will appreciate the option. It is important to remember that while the garden must appeal to adults, it must also be child-friendly and easy to maintain.

You may wish to employ the services of a gardener if your outdoor area is of a substantial size but, if not, it is important that you are able to maintain the property in a short space of time. Bear in mind that you will need to tidy the garden, cut the lawn and water the plants all on the changeover day when the entire house also has to be cleaned and the laundry done! Evergreens and perennial plants are a good choice as they provide year-round colour with the minimum of effort. Window boxes and plants pots, while creating a dramatic visual impact, can be very hard work and, if your guests fail to water them, they will quickly die off. If you do want to use these, consider buying compost and slow-releasing gels and crystals that retain water.

Think about providing the following in the garden or outdoor area:

✓ Table and chairs – sufficient to accommodate the maximum number of guests

✓ Parasol and base
✓ Barbecue and cooking utensils
✓ Playground equipment
✓ Dustbins with lids

If you have a small garden or a patio area and have decided against pots and tubs of flowering plants from a practicality point of view, try brightening the space up with a few well-chosen garden ornaments. Garden centres sell a huge selection of resin, stone and cane ornaments at reasonable prices which are designed to withstand even the harshest winters and these will provide a focal point for your outdoor area. Be warned – plastic gnomes are not advisable!

Child- and pet-friendly properties

If your property is being advertised as welcoming dogs and children, then it is important that you are seen to mean this when furnishing your property and not saying this simply as a way of increasing your bookings. A holiday that accommodates children but has no equipment for them will not go down well with parents! The following are essential for a property that welcomes children:

Babies and young children

- ✓ Cot – this can be a conventional cot or a travel cot with a suitable correctly fitted mattress
- ✓ Highchair with correctly fitted harness
- ✓ Stair gates – sufficient for the number of flights of stairs in the property. A gate should be provided for both the top and the bottom of each flight of stairs.

A nice touch would be to provide a selection of good-quality, clean toys and a selection of melamine or plastic bowls, plates and cups together with suitable cutlery. Feeding bibs can be picked up very cheaply and add the personal touch. All these will help guests to feel that their children really are welcome and not just tolerated!

Pets

Although some guests may request to bring their cat, hamster or even rabbit, the most common pets to holiday with their owners are dogs.

Many people choose holiday accommodation in this country on the basis that they can bring their dog along with them. If your property is in the countryside with lots of good walks on the doorstep, you will probably get many guests requesting to bring their dog along. Provide a mat and two feeding bowls. Place these bowls in the room that you would like them to stay in, for example the conservatory or the utility room, and most guests will respect your wishes and feed their animals where you have placed the bowls. It is also a good idea to provide a few old towels that guests may use to dry their dogs off with before they enter the house. This will save your carpets, and also reduce the risk of guests using your beautiful Egyptian cotton bath towels for the same purpose!

If you are marketing your property to accommodate children and pets, make them feel welcome by providing the basic equipment.

CHAPTER 5 MARKETING

Grading your property

Setting a realistic price for holiday rent is the key to ensuring high occupancy and satisfied customers who will return again and again. Setting the rent too high will ultimately result in complaints from customers who do not feel they have had value for money. Setting the rent too low will result in loss of income and therefore make your holiday cottage venture unsuccessful. The amount of rent you will be able to charge will depend largely on the grade given to your property.

Using a holiday company

If you decide to pay for the services of an agent to let your cottage for you, it will be their job to grade your property. It is entirely up to you whether you agree with the agent or prefer to market your property at a different price to that recommended. However, it is important to realise that an agent has lots of experience with regard to grading property and will have inspected hundreds of houses. The agent will be able to use past experience as a comparison when setting the grade for your property. Some agents will allow you to set your own pricing structure (providing this is not ridiculous, and they feel happy that they can achieve bookings at your chosen level), while others will insist that you go with their grading and pricing structure.

Always listen to the advice offered by a holiday let agent. They have an immense amount of knowledge and experience and there will be very little they have not seen before!

Using a holiday let company

Holiday let agents each have their own methods of grading property, and the system they use will be explained both to you and to any prospective holiday-makers. The grading system is there to enable customers to make an informed choice on the type of holiday they wish to book. Without grading it would be difficult for customers to have an idea of the facilities on offer or the standard of the accommodation.

Although in today's society a lot of people have access to the internet and can therefore view the accommodation before booking, grading is a good way of helping those people who do not have internet access or those who choose to book their holiday using a brochure. Grading also makes the whole booking procedure much easier, as a prospective holiday-maker can request specific details of high-graded properties if they require luxury or low-graded properties if they prefer basic, low-budget accommodation. The grading system cuts out the need to sift through thousands of holiday properties when perhaps only 50 will be of interest.

The facilities you offer in your accommodation, together with the décor, fixtures and fittings, will all have an impact on the grading your property receives.

Grading systems

Some agencies grade properties using a 'star' grading system. The more stars the property has the more luxurious the accommodation. Others use symbols or numbers that refer to a pricing grid which varies depending on the facilities on offer. An even simpler way is to say in the brochure or on the website exactly what the agent's view of the property is, for example 'Comfortable', 'Good Quality' or 'Outstanding'. Each agency will have its own system and this will be explained to you if you request their services.

Assessing accommodation

The number of guests your accommodation can sleep will also have an impact on the price you will be able to charge. However, this does not necessarily mean that a property sleeping eight people can command a higher rate than one sleeping only four. The internal décor and the number of facilities on offer will be a deciding factor on the rental you request. This is where added luxuries can pay dividends. It is always important to go that little bit further and provide extras to appeal to holiday-makers who will be prepared to pay more for luxury.

Every agency will of course want to ensure that the properties they have on offer meet high standards, as this is their way of generating business. Like you, an agency relies on bookings and satisfied customers returning to them. It is vital that the agency you choose grades your property accurately and commands the best price for the accommodation based on its sleeping arrangements, amenities, facilities and, of course, location. Some companies enlist the English Tourism Council to train their representatives in order that they can accurately assess and grade the properties.

The following is a list of some of the things that may have an impact on the grading your property will receive.

Location

This is probably the most important factor. A property in a good location can ultimately command a higher price than one in a less desirable area. Good locations are:

- ✓ Near to a good beach.
- ✓ A character cottage in a romantic or picturesque setting.
- ✓ A city base, particularly near to London, Edinburgh, York, etc.

Generally, people choosing a holiday property are looking for accommodation that is different to what they have at home. They may be looking for adventure in a converted lighthouse, romance in a thatched, chocolate-box cottage or simply luxury in a manor house with a pool. If, however, your property is a two-bedroomed terraced house in a windswept location do not be deterred. Having a property in a less desirable location may not command maximum rentals but, if you furnish it correctly and add the right amount of quality facilities, you will still be able to find guests wishing to rent it. Your initial task of making the property appeal to holiday-makers may be a little harder with a property in a less desirable area but it is by no means impossible.

Décor and furnishings

It is important that your property does not appear shabby. Often a lick of paint is all that is required to bring a house up to a good standard and can make a huge difference to its grading. Chipped paint and peeling wallpaper will not please customers and these are problems that must be addressed. A dirty worn suite and threadbare carpets will not have the desired impact, nor will poor-quality bed linen and towels, so invest wisely and buy furnishings and linen that will stay looking good.

Fixtures and fittings

A lot of people are loathe to spend vast amounts of money on new kitchens and bathrooms in a property that is being rented out. However, it is always a good idea to invest in quality fixtures and fittings. They need not be the most expensive but by paying a little bit more and settling for a mid-range rather than a budget range will pay dividends in the long run. Not only will the quality be obvious, but the fixtures and fittings will stand the test of time and stay looking good for longer.

When choosing fixtures and fittings it is worth bearing in mind that short-term lets to holiday-makers are generally a safer bet than long-term lets in terms of your property being cared for. There is, of course, always an exception to every rule, but I am of the opinion that people on holiday, while they may not spring-clean the property, are usually happy to look after the house and its contents, and in my experience short-term lets do not seem to get the same abuse as those that are long-term.

Facilities

People on holiday are usually looking for a home from home but with added luxuries. For example, someone who does not own a dishwasher will be impressed to find one at their holiday accommodation. Generally, anything that will make life easier will be a welcome addition to the property. An automatic washing machine, tumble dryer and teasmaid would be worthwhile investments. Other facilities which may increase your property's grading would be a freezer (in addition to a fridge), cable television, music system, games consoles, etc.

Properties with luxuries such as a gym, snooker room or a swimming pool will almost definitely be able to command maximum rental, provided of course that the rest of the property is up to standard.

Choosing an agent

When choosing a company to market and let your property, it is important that you request details first to read at your leisure, so that you are confident you have chosen the right company. Some companies concentrate on certain areas of the country and may refuse to take on a property outside their preferred location. Others prefer only character cottages in romantic settings. It is important to shop around before choosing an agent. Letting agencies differ and each one will offer its own incentive. Get a feel for the company by browsing their website and seeing how many bookings they have generated for the properties they are already marketing. Look at the different grading and pricing structures and of course be aware of the costs and charges incurred for the company's services.

A good agency will offer help and support both prior to your property being advertised and after. It is important for the agency you choose to be confident that the property is of a good standard and that it will generate lots of bookings.

When you have decided on which agency to use, someone from the company will visit you at your holiday let property to assess the accommodation and advise you of the best way you can maximise its potential. They will explain their company's grading and pricing systems and inform you of how much they feel they could market your property for. They should be able to advise you of added purchases you may like to make or suggest changes that could make the property more appealing to holiday-makers. They should not be seen to be criticising your property. However, it is important that you take on board the advice you are offered and remember the representative will have seen hundreds, possibly thousands, of properties and they are in an excellent position to compare your holiday home to others they have inspected. They should be aware of what sells and what doesn't and will be able to give you sound help and advice.

If you are completely in the dark about the best way to furnish and decorate your property, try speaking to your chosen agency *before* you make any major decisions or purchases. They may well be able to come out to the property, in advance, to advise you of what to buy in order to reach the property's maximum potential. For example, would you buy bunk beds for a small bedroom or would you opt for one single bed? Bunk beds may well accommodate another guest but is this feasible in your particular property? My own experience, using a particular agency, paid dividends. I telephoned the company ahead of the date I was hoping to market my property. They took details from me and sent their regional manager out. My property was by no means finished but the manager was able to give me lots of helpful advice. I told her my plans and she then explained whether or not she thought these ideas would be beneficial as far as rental potential was concerned. I was pleased to have been able to speak to her while still in the planning stage as she prevented me from making expensive purchases that would have seen little, if any, return in rental.

> Don't assume your property must be completed and ready to let before contacting an agent. Often an agency will send someone out to the property ahead of schedule to offer help and advice on furnishing and décor.

The biggest advantage of employing the services of a holiday let agency is without a doubt the marketing facilities they have to offer. When choosing which agency to use, always bear in mind the company's marketing facilities. Opt for a company that can give your property maximum exposure and therefore ensure plenty of bookings. You may have purchased a dream property and furnished it to a very high standard, but unless you or your agent market the property successfully you may never get the desired number of bookings. Ask the agency how they propose to market your property and how much they usually spend on marketing and advertising properties each year. Look at the brochures they produce: are they of good quality, are they easy to understand, do they show properties to their maximum potential? Does the agency have a website? If so, is it easy to use and does it give plenty of useful information? What other distribution channels does the company have? Choosing a well-known company with a large advertising budget will probably be your safest bet. Ask yourself an important question that most holiday-makers will also consider:

Would you book a holiday with a well-known company before one that you haven't heard of?

Most people would invariably opt for the well-known company as they feel safe in the knowledge that the company has experience and they are confident that if things go wrong they have a reliable agency to turn to.

That is not to say that a smaller company will not be a good choice. Sometimes a more personal service can be had by going with a small company and holiday-makers may take this into consideration. However, as someone employing the services of an agent it is vital that you opt for a company that will work for *you*. In addition to a large advertising budget, you must also look at the services they provide. Help and advice is usually free but you may also like to look at the company's administration system. Ask them about their booking procedure and the paperwork they provide. How do they take bookings and collect payments? When can you expect to see any money? How do they handle complaints? What happens in the event of a cancellation? All these questions are vital to the smooth running of a holiday let property and it is important that you enquire what, if any, services the agency provides. You may be required to deal with any complaints yourself, for example, and this is one area where you would probably need the agency's help and advice. Don't assume that all agencies will offer assistance with all aspects of running your letting business.

Some companies offer a complete package, including advertising, administration, support and advice, housekeeping, insurance and accountancy. If you are intending to leave everything up to your agency, then it is vital that you check beforehand that they provide all the services you require and at what cost. If you have the time and the inclination you can save yourself money by doing some of the things yourself. For example, if you live near to the property you could do your own changeover cleans and laundry and therefore save yourself the expense of employing a housekeeper or using the agency's cleaning services. If you are familiar with accounts and book-keeping you may find it relatively easy to do your own accounts and tax returns, saving yourself the expense of employing an accountant. The agency you choose depends very much on how much work you intend to put into your holiday let venture.

What to look for in an agency

In short, some of the important factors you should consider when choosing a holiday let agency are:

1. A proven history in the holiday let market where maximum booking potential is achieved.
2. Extensive advertising on a national level.
3. A good marketing strategy.
4. Financial protection – advance payments and cancellation protection.
5. Freedom for personal bookings – some agencies may prevent you from using your holiday cottage yourself throughout the busy summer season. Check that the company you are intending to use does not charge penalties for owner bookings.
6. Internet access with virtual tours.
7. Owner support.
8. Quality administration service.
9. Housekeeping service.
10. Accountancy service.

To help you to decide which, if any, holiday let agency you should choose, we will now look at some of the companies and what they have to offer.

Holiday Cottages Group Limited. This company consists of several brands that make up Cendant VRG (UK). Three of the well-known holiday let agencies within this group are:

Country Holidays

I have always found this company to offer an excellent service. They have a very high level of customer satisfaction and offer 25 years of knowledge and expertise. Country Holidays have an annual marketing budget that exceeds £3 million. Their advertisements feature in national newspapers, holiday and national interest magazines, and Tourist Board publications. The company is well known and offers a colourful, glossy brochure with an extensive distribution reaching over 4 million potential customers, together with website access and virtual tours of many of their properties.

Country Holidays can handle up to 8,000 telephone calls per day and they have over 100 telephone lines. Their sales advisors are highly trained and have access to computer software that can immediately offer a customer alternative accommodation, should their first choice be unavailable.

Rental money is paid directly into the owner's bank account, in advance, and monthly statements are issued, together with booking details as and when they are taken. Protection against cancellation is also offered and Country Holidays recognise that holiday home owners may wish to use the property themselves. They therefore agree to allow a set number of weeks per year for owner bookings, which will be detailed on your contract. For further information about Country Holidays, visit their website: www.country-holidays.co.uk

Welcome Cottages

Again, this company has a large marketing budget and regularly appears in all the major national daily and Sunday newspapers together with many specialist magazines, including *The National Trust*, *Dog World* and *Birds Magazine*. Welcome Cottages reaches a wide audience and they distribute over 2.5 million brochures every year. Like most other companies, Welcome Cottages charge an annual registration fee, and they are happy for owners to withdraw their property for their own use providing they follow the company's guidelines for the number of weeks and notice given.

Welcome Cottages offer a superb range of holiday properties throughout the United Kingdom and Ireland. For more information, visit their website: www.welcomeowner.com

English Country Cottages

This company was set up in 1977 and since then it has become one of the largest rental agencies in the market. English Country Cottages advertise their properties in England and Wales and also incorporate additional brochures that include Scottish, Irish, French and Italian country cottages.

English Country Cottages state that almost three-quarters of their visitors are in the upper income brackets and that, rather than trying to compete with overseas holidays, their company complements them, as their average customer takes two or more holidays per year.

English Country Cottages advertise widely in the major national newspapers, quality periodicals, women's magazines and special interest publications. They also offer a full overseas promotion service and generate bookings from over 15 different countries, including mainland Europe, Australia and New Zealand, South Africa and the United States. Further information about English Country Cottages can be found on their website: www.english-country-cottages.co.uk

Recommended Cottage Holidays are based in North Yorkshire and offer holiday cottages throughout the country.

They employ trained staff and are open seven days a week to answer queries and take bookings. Like other companies, they advertise in the national press and through tourist information centres, travel agents and overseas agents. Recommended Cottage Holidays offer a unique owner booking policy, whereby owners of holiday homes can book as many weeks as they like and will not incur any commission charges. All the company ask is that you keep them informed of your personal use or your own bookings in order that they can be sure they do not double book. This is a great advantage to holiday home owners who frequently use their own property, as many other companies either charge a commission for owner bookings or restrict the number of owner bookings allowed. Recommended Cottage Holidays advertise their properties and computer booking system on the internet and payments are made to owners for the bookings monthly in advance. More information can be found on their website: www.recommended-cottages.co.uk.

Things to consider when choosing your agent

There is no shortage of holiday let agencies in Britain, so it is important to do your homework and choose wisely. Think about:

1. The advertising scope.
2. The particular areas of the country that the agency concentrates on. If your property is in Wales there is little point trying to market it with a company that specialises in the Scottish Highlands.
3. The type of property the agency already has on its books. If you have a standard cottage aimed at budget holiday-makers, it will not benefit you to put your property with an agency that caters largely for the discerning customer looking for a luxury holiday in a top-of-the-range property. Even if the agency agreed

to take your property (which is highly unlikely), you would probably end up with a lot of dissatisfied customers and a lengthy list of complaints.

4. The advice and services offered. Some companies will offer housekeeping and gardening services while others will expect you to find your own. Bear in mind that agencies usually charge a premium for these services, and you would be well advised to find your own maintenance staff if you are not able to clean and maintain the property yourself.

5. The commission charges the company takes. Make sure the percentage taken by the agency is not extortionate and that the service they provide justifies the commission they command.

In theory, using a holiday let agency should remove all the hassle and worry associated with the promotion, marketing, administration and letting of your holiday home. They should also ensure that payments are received on time and work with you to solve any problems or complaints. All agents offer different services. When choosing which agent to advertise your property with, avoid selecting the one that demands the highest rental. Although in theory you should expect to make more money from higher rentals, this is not always the case with holiday let agencies, as the extra commission they charge may cancel out any profits made. You must take into consideration the things the agency has to offer and whether or not they are of benefit to you *personally* as a holiday home owner. If you have no intention of using the property yourself and simply wish to rent the property out for as many weeks as possible, then there is no point in selecting an agency that offers numerous free weeks, free of commission charges, to the owners, unless of course you are able to generate plenty of bookings yourself through friends, family, work colleagues, etc., in which case this may be worth considering.

In general, the most important aspect to think about when choosing your agent is their means to promote your property. A well-established agency with a good customer database and an excellent reputation will probably do your property justice. Check the advertising methods the agency uses and the number of bookings they aim to achieve. Be prepared to pay slightly more for a well-established agency but bear in mind that their expertise and success in marketing and generating bookings may well be worth paying a little extra for in commission charges.

There are several agencies that specialise in certain properties. They may be much smaller but do consider them if they offer a unique service for the type of property you own or its location. For example, a company specialising in cottages in the Yorkshire Dales would be a good consideration if you own a barn conversion in Ingleton. Likewise, a company specialising in city holidays would be ideal for someone hoping to let a flat in central London.

The key is to shop around and, once again, be prepared to do your homework. You may decide on a particular agency but, after the initial enquiry, realise that they are not offering what you are looking for, or indeed find that they are not interested in your property. (This can and does happen if a company specialises in certain properties and yours is not up to the required specification.)

Marketing the property yourself

Of course it is not essential that you use the services of an agent to market your property, though if you wish to generate maximum bookings then using an agent will almost definitely be your best bet initially. Before deciding to market the property yourself, you must consider a number of points:

1. Are you only intending to let your property to family and friends? If this is the case, then you will probably be fine producing and distributing a simple leaflet.

2. Are you intending to generate bookings throughout the year to help you pay the costs of owning your property? If so:

   a) How do you intend to market your property?

   b) What is your advertising budget?

3. Are you able to take enquiries and distribute details of your holiday home?

4. Are you able to collect payments?

5. Will you be on hand to deal with any problems or complaints?

You must answer these questions realistically. You may well be able to deal with all the enquiries and administration involved in the running of a holiday home if you work part-time or work from home, but how will you take bookings and answer queries if you work long hours or shift patterns? Research carried out by holiday let agencies has shown that the majority of customers book their holidays at the weekend or evenings, probably because this is the time the family spends together and they are able to take into account everyone's preferences when choosing the holiday destination. Therefore, if you work weekends or evenings you will not be in a position to take bookings, and your holiday let business will almost certainly suffer because of it.

When first letting a holiday cottage it is probably true to say that most owners feel anxious during the first few lettings. I think all holiday property owners have sat down and thought, 'What opinion will customers have of my property?', 'Will they hate the area, house, etc.?' We all want our customers to have a fantastic holiday, love the property, return time and time again and tell their friends and family. This is of course how to make your holiday let business successful and generate a good rental income. If this is the case, and I sincerely hope it is, and you have lots of happy, satisfied customers, resist the urge to dispense with your agency's services straight away. On looking at your statement you won't help but notice the commission fees charged by the agency and many people think that they will benefit greatly by going it alone, dropping the agency, and doing all the work themselves. However, you must ask yourself how practical this would be. Your biggest problem will be finding the customers. You may have had half a dozen satisfied customers to date but it is unrealistic to expect them all to return every year and tell their friends and family about your property.

So, unless you have a means of reaching a large number of potential customers, I would advise you to retain the services of your agent for at least a couple of years. This way you will be able to build up a good client database from past bookings. Your agency will furnish you with the names and contact addresses of all the people who use your property and you can then contact these people and offer them the chance to book a holiday directly with you. You could offer an incentive by telling them that the property is cheaper now that you don't require the help of an agency. Even if you reduce the property by, say, £50.00 per week you will probably still be earning more money than you did when customers booked through the agency, as the commission fees you paid to them are likely to have been higher than this.

By booking directly with the owner, customers also save the booking fee that most agencies charge. All in all, potential customers stand to save in excess of £100 per booking, often much more, if they book directly with the owner.

Contacting previous customers

Before contacting previous customers, it is important that you read your contract carefully, as some agencies include clauses restricting you from bypassing them and depriving them of their commission fees. If you are thinking of doing this, it is important to make sure you do not sign a contract that forbids you from contacting past customers. It may be wise to employ a solicitor who could advise you whether or not the clause is legally enforceable, and to ask yourself whether or not the company is likely to pursue it. It is impossible for an agency to forbid you to contact previous customers forever, so it may just be necessary to wait a reasonable length of time before pursuing them.

It is worth remembering that however you decide to market your property, either by yourself or through an agent, the single most important factor that will enable your future selling strategy to work is your past customers. If your guests have enjoyed themselves and had a good holiday, they are likely to tell their friends and family.

A good way of contacting previous customers is to send them a Christmas card and enclose your property brochure and price list. Guests who have holidayed in your property in the past may well have forgotten how much they enjoyed their stay, and a reminder is all they need to encourage them to repeat the experience.

REMEMBER

If you let your property for 25 weeks of the year for two years with an agency you will have reached 50 customers. If each of these customers tells ten others about their enjoyable holiday, you have a potential customer database of 500! This number will be increased with every year you keep your property with an agency. When you feel the time is right and you have a substantial list of potential customers, you may like to try to market the property yourself.

Whatever you decide, whether you stay with an agency or go it alone you must always bear in mind how much work is involved in successfully marketing a property. Don't look at your agent's commission fee as wasted money – they are providing you with a valuable service and generating customers as well as offering expert advice. Resist the temptation to be greedy. Do you really have the time, energy and patience to do all the work yourself just to save a few hundred pounds?

If you do decide to go it alone and take on the task of marketing the property yourself there are some very important things that you need to consider:

Advertising

How are you intending to advertise your property? An agent is likely to have a budget of thousands, possibly millions, of pounds to spend on advertising and can therefore reach a wide audience. You, on the other hand, will probably have a limited amount of money to spend on advertising your holiday property and it is therefore important to spend this money wisely. Think about how much you wish to spend and when and where you are going to advertise. If you work in a big company and have a lot of colleagues, you may like to start there, perhaps by placing a flyer on the notice board. Friends and family are also a good place to start, although it is important to remember that unless you have a huge family and an endless supply of friends who go on holiday often, you are unlikely to make a lot of money from the people you know. Often friends and family will expect to holiday in your property at a reduced fee or, even worse, free of charge. Make sure that your family and friends are aware that you are hoping to use your property as a business venture and therefore make money from it.

You will need to prepare a flyer or small brochure to send out to potential customers who enquire about your property. If you have a camera and the use of a computer and are reasonably confident, you should be able to prepare a brochure yourself. You will need to include a short description of the property, the number of people it sleeps, its location, availability and price list, together with your telephone number for people to contact should they wish to book. Try to keep the brochure simple and on as few sheets of paper as possible in order to make it cost-effective. Remember there will be a percentage of your brochures that will end up in the dustbin!

It is a good idea, if you have the knowledge, to prepare a website to advertise your holiday property. A large number of people use websites to source and book their holidays.

If you are not confident that you have the ability to produce a brochure or website for your property, you may like to instruct someone to do this for you. Remember that you will have to pay for this service and, although it may be a one-off payment, it will eat into your advertising budget. It is a good idea to produce a price list separate to your brochure which you can insert. This will enable you to increase or amend your prices as and when necessary, without the need to reproduce the entire brochure, therefore cutting down on costs.

In addition to notice boards at work, you must think about other places to advertise your holiday property. National newspapers are very expensive and it is therefore unlikely that this will be an option. Local newspapers are much cheaper but even these can add up if you are intending to advertise your property on a regular basis. Posters and leaflets in shop windows may generate a small amount of business, although this method is unlikely to attract sufficient customers to enable your holiday let business to be a success and make a decent profit.

It may be a good idea to put a poster in the window of the property itself, when it is empty, advertising itself as a holiday let. However, like posters in shop windows, this will only reach customers who are already familiar with the area and not potential customers searching for a new destination.

Below is an example of a brochure/website page for a holiday property. The details can be altered to suit either a brochure to send to potential customers or a webpage.

HAVERIGG HOLIDAYS

HOME

Home

About Us

Contact Us

A holiday home by the sea in Haverigg.

The house is situated on the sea wall in Haverigg, a small village, in south-west Cumbria.

The property has three bedrooms (one double, one twin and one single) and two bathrooms, and it can accommodate five guests.

There is a newly fitted kitchen, lounge with dining area and a conservatory.

A small enclosed patio garden with furniture is situated at the rear of the property.

The beach is just a few yards from the property and there are breathtaking views over the surrounding fells and countryside.

The popular towns of Bowness and Coniston are approximately 30 minutes away by car.

FOR MORE INFORMATION, AVAILABILITY AND PRICES, PLEASE CONTACT:

Your Address
Your Telephone Number
Your Email Address

Selling

Are you good at selling? If you decide to market the property yourself rather than through an agent, you will need to make the most of every opportunity. Whenever you receive an enquiry from a potential customer you will need to sell your property to the best of your ability in order to ensure regular bookings. *Never* be tempted to lie about your property in order to make it sound better than it really is, as this will only result in disappointment and complaints if the property is not up to the standard you have described. If you have done your homework well, chosen a good area, a suitable property and furnished it to a decent standard, you will not need to exaggerate its potential in order to secure bookings. Concentrate on the property's good points and use your knowledge of the area and the facilities to inform prospective holiday-makers of what your property has to offer. Make sure the person enquiring about your property *wants* to book before your telephone conversation is over.

In order to maximise booking potential, it is vital that you are available when customers want to book. Think about the hours you work and the times you will be available to answer the telephone and take bookings or send details. The vast majority of holiday-makers tend to confer with their partners or families about their preferred destinations and therefore weekends and evenings tend to be popular times for enquiries and bookings. Are you available during these times? If not, consider giving out an alternative telephone number on which you can be contacted, perhaps your business number if this is appropriate. Missed enquiries and bookings should be avoided at all costs!

Administration

Another important factor to consider, which will inevitably take up a good deal of your time, is administration. In addition to mailing brochures and taking bookings, you will need to think about your ability to:

1. Organise a booking system that is simple and easy to use, so that you do not miss bookings or double book.

2. Develop a system for cancellations.

3. Handle complaints.

4. Organise a system to handle payments. Will you have credit card payment facilities or will you only accept cheques? Will you request initial deposits with payment in full before or after the customer has taken their holiday? Think about how you will chase up payments if they are not forthcoming or if the cheque bounces.

5. Organise a system whereby you can accept weekly rentals, short breaks and weekends.

6. Handle situations whereby guests have caused damage to your property.

7. Decide whether or not you will accept pets, and if so, how many and will you charge extra for them? How will you monitor the number of pets clients take?

8. Provide the facilities required to run a holiday let business yourself. Ideally you will have at the very least a computer with email connection and a telephone. A filing cabinet, stationery and fax machine may also be worth considering. It is probably true to say that most customers prefer to book a holiday through a reputable company and by marketing your property yourself you will already be alienating some of your potential customers, so it is vital that you show professionalism to the people who are considering booking with you direct. The price of a holiday let can vary considerably depending on the size and location of the property. A week's rental can be anything from a couple of hundred pounds up to a thousand pounds or more. Would you be happy handing over £1,000 to someone who is often unavailable and provides a shabby brochure and correspondence scribbled on a

scrap of paper? You will need to send out letters, booking confirmations, payment requests, receipts, property directions, etc., and all these should be presented in a clear, professional way. Your customers will expect the same service from you as they would from an agency and it is up to you not to disappoint.

Accounts

Although you may wish to market your property yourself, it may still be worth considering the services of an account-ant if you are not familiar with the system or you are unaware of the advantages on offer. The financial aspect of running a holiday let company is covered in greater detail in Chapter 10 of this book.

Before deciding to market your property yourself, it is vital that you consider all of the above points. You will invari-ably save money if you decide against using an agent; however, if you weigh up the amount of money you save with the considerable amount of time you will have to devote to your holiday let business, you may well decide the saving is not worth it. Sometimes it is worth paying an agent, particularly in the early days when potential cus-tomers are thin on the ground and you have little experience. While every property is different, and every area has something unique to offer, so too has each prop-erty owner. Some people may love managing a holiday let themselves and enjoy the selling and paperwork involved, while others may be filled with dread. The type of person *you* are will help you to decide whether to go it alone or employ an agent.

Advertising

Although we have already looked at advertising briefly in this chapter, it is important to remember that advertising is probably the single most important aspect of running a holiday let business. Without a decent advertising strategy you will have no means of reaching potential customers and will therefore achieve very few bookings and limited rental money. Whether you decide to market your property yourself or place it in the hands of an agent, advertising will play a huge part in whether or not your property is successful as a holiday let.

If you decide to employ an agent, the advertising side of things will be largely out of your hands. However, before selecting which agent to use it is paramount that you familiarise yourself with the agent's marketing strategy and that you are happy with this. As well as using a holiday let agency, you may also like to advertise the property yourself, with your own contact details, in order to maximise the number of bookings. However, if you choose to do this, make sure there are no restrictions in the contract you have with your agent and, most importantly, that you do not double book your property. In addition to national and local newspapers, you may also like to consider the following ways to advertise your holiday property:

- ✓ **Tourist Information Centres** Enquire at your local centres about the possibility of placing a few leaflets with them. Often Tourist Information Centres are potential holiday-makers' first ports of call and you may well generate business this way.

- ✓ **Tourist Boards** You may need to register as a member and pay an annual fee, but for this you will get your property entered in their brochure and on their official website. Finding a holiday property through Tourist Boards is still a very popular method with a lot of holiday-makers and the relatively low cost involved makes this a marketing strategy well worth considering.

- ✓ **Specialist magazines** For example, if your accommodation is in the Yorkshire Dales, try placing an advert in the *Dalesman*. Likewise, a property in

Cumbria could be placed in the *Cumbria and Lake District Magazine*. A property that offers excellent fishing, golf or water sports may benefit from an advert placed in a publication aimed at these particular interests.

✓ **Local shops and Post Office windows** Try advertising both where the property is situated and in your own local shops. It may be worth sending one or two leaflets to surrounding areas or to similar places that are perhaps already heavily populated or expensive. For example, a property in a quiet area in Cumbria may benefit from having an advert placed in the shop window of a nearby bustling town or village such as Coniston or Windermere. Describe the property and its closeness to the town you have selected to place the advert in, and make sure you do your homework and advertise your property cheaper than those found in the areas you are competing with. You will be surprised how many people are happy to drive for 20 minutes to their ideal destination during the day if they can save money on their holiday accommodation.

✓ **The internet** If you are serious about marketing your property yourself, you really must consider advertising your property on the internet. Placing an advert on the web will enable you to reach a huge number of potential customers. There are two ways of going about advertising on the internet. You can either:

Pay a professional website designer to produce a webpage for you, though this can prove expensive as you will incorporate the following costs:

1. The initial cost of the website.
2. Further costs if you wish to update or alter your site, which you will probably need to do annually if you put your rental rates on.

3. Registration fees payable every two years.

4. Host fees usually paid every year.

Or you could:

Look into the possibility of placing an advert with other holiday property owners and share the costs. Remember though that by doing this you may be competing with several other people and the advantages of saving on internet set-up costs may be outweighed by this competition.

If you do decide to place your property on the internet, it is important to make sure you include the following information:

1. Good-quality digital photographs. Show at least one good photograph of the outside of the property and its surrounding area. You may like to put other photographs on your webpage showing the inside of the property. If you have a luxury master bedroom with a four-poster bed, then this would be a good feature to advertise.

2. The location of your property. Make sure you do not put the exact address on your webpage as there is the possibility that this may attract unsavoury characters looking for a property which may well be empty.

3. A brief description of the property. For example, a beachside haven situated yards from a glorious sandy beach, or a seventeenth-century thatched cottage in the heart of a picturesque village.

4. The number of bedrooms the property has and how many guests it can accommodate. Briefly list the bedroom set-up, i.e. two double bedrooms, one twin, and one cot.

5. A brief description of the rooms available and the facilities provided. Include any luxuries your property features, such as a whirlpool bath, dishwasher, games console, snooker table or swimming pool. Also mention any outside area the property has, and if this is suitable for entertaining and barbecues.

6. The availability of the property.

7. A price list showing low, mid and high season.

8. The changeover details, whether the property is let Saturday to Saturday or Sunday to Sunday.

9. Whether or not you accept weekend or midweek short breaks.

10. Your contact details. If you are out during the day, add available times for customers to contact you next to your telephone number.

✓ **Word of mouth** This is always a good marketing strategy, not least because it is free. Tell friends and family and offer an incentive to them if they help you to secure a booking by telling their friends about your property. You will be surprised how many people you can reach this way. Take a few minutes to write down how many friends you can name, add to these how many members of your family there are and then multiply this number by, say, ten for the people they may tell and already you have got a large number of potential customers to aim at.

If the area where your property is situated has an annual carnival or celebration day, consider increasing your advertising strategy during this period as it is likely to generate more interest and additional visitors.

Another advertising strategy you may like to consider is offering a week's holiday at your property as a prize. Try your local school's summer or Christmas fair. This could well be a good way of selling raffle tickets to help the school, as well as another way of reaching potential customers. Never forget that every person who knows about your property has the potential of telling dozens of others. Word of mouth is an advertising strategy which should never be underestimated.

Deciding how much to charge

If you employ the services of an agency, deciding how much to charge for your holiday accommodation may well be out of your hands. However, a decent agency should ask you what kind of income you are hoping to achieve and work with you to decide on the best rental fees. Always take notice of what your agent has to say and heed their advice. They will have years of experience and will have seen dozens of properties and will therefore be in a good position to know the market and have an idea of which kinds of property can command certain amounts of rent.

If you have decided to market your property yourself, you must think long and hard before setting your rental fees. There will be several factors you will need to take into account:

1. **Your mortgage** If you have a mortgage on the property, you may well want your rental to be high enough to cover your mortgage payments.

2. **Caretaking** If you are employing the services of a cleaner and/or gardener, you should take into account the wages you will have to pay for these services when calculating your rental.

3. **Gas/electricity/water** If you have decided to charge an 'all inclusive' rental, you must incorporate the cost of these services in your rent.

4. **Special facilities** If your property offers any special facilities such as a swimming pool, which will incorporate additional charges for heating and cleaning, make sure you add a proportion of these fees to your rental.

5. **Pets** Are you going to allow guests to bring dogs into your property? If so, it is standard practice to charge extra for this as you will probably incur more cleaning expenses. An average cost for accommodating dogs is approximately £15–£20 per pet per week.

6. **Laundry** Are you intending to charge extra for towels and bedding or will this price be reflected in the weekly rental?

7. **Competition** How many other similar properties are there in your area offering holiday accommodation? Enquire about their rental fees and bear these in mind when setting your own.

All of the above must be taken into consideration when setting your fees. In addition to covering some of the basic overheads listed above, remember also that you will have other costs such as insurance, decorating, carpet cleaning and general house repairs to think about, and a percentage of all of these should be included in the rent so that the property is in effect 'paying for itself'. It is of little use running a property let business if your outgoings for the upkeep of the property are far higher than the income you are receiving. In addition to ensuring that the property pays for itself, you should also be aiming to make a profit from your business. You may be happy for all of your overheads to be covered, particularly if you have a mortgage on the property and are not looking for a reasonable cash profit besides. You will probably be expecting your property to go up in value and therefore increase your investment over the long term. If, however, you only have a small mortgage or no mortgage at all on the property, you should be looking to reap some financial benefit from your letting business, if only to cover the time and expense you have put into marketing your venture. The amount of money you make will, of course, not only be dependent on the rent you can charge but also on the number of bookings you are able to secure.

Even if you decide against using the services of an agent, you would be best advised to request several of their brochures in order to get an idea of the rentals they charge. Sift through the brochures for properties that accommodate the same number of guests as your property, in similar areas, and familiarise yourself with the amount of rent each company is commanding for each month of the year. Remember that agents take a cut from the prices shown in the brochures and these can sometimes be as much as a third or even half of the costs quoted. You should be able to use the rental fees quoted in agency brochures as a guideline to the amount of rent you can reasonably expect to achieve. Bear in mind that people are often willing to pay more for a holiday through an agency, as they feel happier and more secure knowing that they have booked through a reputable company. If, however, you can prove that you are a serious property owner offering a professional service at a lower price, you may well attract customers.

Try to work on a strategy similar to the one below.

Property A three-bedroom property sleeping five people near the beach could well command the following rental through an agency:

Low season	£195.00
Mid season	£341.00
High season	£431.00

A property owner advertising their house through the agency at these rents may only see the following income, after the agency has deducted their fees:

Low season	£128.00
Mid season	£228.00
High season	£308.00

The agency in this case has taken a cut of between £67.00 and £123.00 per week for their services. If you chose to market your property yourself, you could afford to reduce the rental charged to the customer by between £40 and £80 per week, depending on the season, making your property a more attractive proposition while still ensuring a larger weekly profit than you would through an agency.

Remember, these figures are only an estimate and you must bear in mind that the type and location of the property will ultimately be the deciding factor as to how much you can reasonably expect to charge. A chocolate-box detached cottage with a thatched roof in the heart of the Cotswolds could well command in excess of £700 per week, depending on the number of people it accommodates and the time of year it is being rented out.

Although it may seem like 'easy money' to cut out the agent and make more profit yourself, this will only work if you have a good customer database or an excellent means of marketing your property.

REMEMBER

One of the most important jobs you are paying an agent to do is to advertise and promote your property to the largest number of potential customers possible. Without the bookings, neither you nor your agent will make any profit!

Charging for extras

Most people who are planning to book a holiday have a budget in mind. The weekly rental that you are asking for your property should, wherever possible, include as many extras as is reasonable. Once a customer has booked their holiday, they are usually unwilling to fork out extra money for gas, electricity, bedding, towels, etc. so aim to offer your property at 'all-inclusive' prices. If you choose to promote your property through an agency, they may well have restrictions on the number of extras you are allowed to charge for, as experience has taught them that customers do not like paying additional costs.

It is therefore vital that you incorporate any extra costs you may incur by letting your property into the rental fees that you charge. Take into account:

1. The amount of gas and electricity that may be used. Obviously this will be higher in the winter months when guests are more likely to need to heat the property.
2. Your housekeeper's wages, if you choose to employ the services of a cleaner.
3. A gardener's wages, if you choose to employ one.
4. Laundry costs for washing and drying bedding and towels.
5. Window cleaner.

It is widely acceptable to charge an extra amount of rental if the guests wish to bring along their pets. This is because there is usually more cleaning involved after they have left, for example, pet hairs to eradicate. Most agencies accept this and also charge extra for pets. Whether you are marketing the property yourself or through an agent, I would not recommend that you charge more than, say, £20.00 per pet, and less if possible. Most agencies will set the amount payable for pets, but if you are marketing the property yourself, be aware that some guests may want to bring more than one dog and the 'extras' can easily add up and put them off booking. Although you may incur extra costs for cleaning, it is probably true to say that £20.00 will more than cover the cost of the extra vacuuming.

Decide how many pets you are going to allow guests to bring and state this in the holiday let information, either with your agency or in your own brochure. Some people prefer to allow only one small, well-behaved pet while others will allow several. Think about the size and space your property has to offer before deciding on the number of pets you will allow.

It is also worth bearing in mind that some dogs leave behind a strong odour, and it is vital that you air your property well after guests with dogs have left and before the new guests arrive.

How long is the holiday season?

This is not an easy question to answer, as it simply depends on the location of the property. While some properties can only expect bookings throughout the summer months and are best taken off the market and closed up for the winter, others may well command bookings 52 weeks of the year. In addition to the location of the property, another factor that will affect the number of weeks' bookings will be the price and what this includes, for example, gas, electric, linen and towels. It is probably true to say that even if you offered the accommodation free of charge in November and February, some properties would still remain empty due to their location. Very remote country properties, though tranquil in summer, are often completely inaccessible in the winter months!

On average, agencies would tell you that experience has taught them that the average property can expect between 25 and 35 bookings per annum with the most prestigious properties reaching between 40 and 50 bookings. This will of course depend on the agent you choose and their methods of advertising. Some agencies offer properties at a reduced rate for late bookings in order to achieve maximum occupancy. I would advise you to steer clear of any agency that cannot fill your property during the most popular summer months of June, July and August. Any agency with a good marketing strategy should have no trouble generating bookings during this time of the year.

If your property is not popular during the winter months do not despair, as often the rental achieved during the summer is sufficient to cover the property's annual costs. If you are marketing the property yourself do not appear too desperate to secure winter bookings by undercharging, as you may well end up out of pocket. Although it is true to say that the rent you charge in the winter will be less than the summer, make sure that the money you do receive covers the cost of the additional heating in the colder months, as well as any cleaning involved. If you employ a housekeeper, the fees you pay for this service will be the same regardless of how much you receive in rental.

There is little point in letting your property for a week and charging £100 in rent if the housekeeper and fuel charges amount to more than the figure you have charged. Making a loss is not an option. However, making *less profit* in the winter is seriously worth considering, if only because your house is not left empty for many months. The property will be aired and, from a security point of view, would be better rented as much as possible throughout the year.

CHAPTER 6

BOOKINGS

Deposit and balances

The amount of administration and accountancy involved in your business will be dependent on whether you employ the services of an agent or decide to do the work yourself.

If you employ an agent, they will be responsible for taking your bookings. A deposit will usually be requested at the time of the booking and this can be anything from, say, £50 per week to a percentage of the overall cost of the rental. Most holiday let agencies request the balance of the monies due eight to ten weeks before the date the holiday is to be taken. If you decide not to employ the services of an agent, then the taking of deposits and balances will lie solely with you. This may seem like an easy quest, but you should bear in mind that some guests may fail to pay the balance on time, or cancel at the last minute, and you should have a strategy in place for dealing with these situations.

When deciding on the amount of deposit to charge, bear in mind the following:

1. Too high a deposit may put off potential customers, particularly those who are already wary of booking directly with an owner rather than through an agent.

2. Too low a deposit may enable the potential guests to cancel at the last minute, as they do not risk losing a large amount of money. If they cancel within a couple of weeks of when their holiday is due to commence, it may be difficult for you to re-book the property. You therefore stand to lose a large sum of money should this happen in the prime weeks throughout the summer season. If you advertise your holiday property for £500 for a week in August and only request potential customers to pay a £20 deposit, if they cancel at the last minute you stand to lose £480 in potential rental. Of course, if you are able to re-book the property you stand to make the extra £20 in profit.

3. If you try to overcome the potential for cancellations by requesting that customers pay an additional amount should they cancel within, say, four weeks of departure, it is highly unlikely that you will receive the money. Of course, cancelling a holiday is in some cases inevitable, but for others it may just be because of the lack of funds or a change of heart. You should try to set your deposits at a level that you are happy with in the unfortunate circumstances that someone may have to cancel.

If you employ an agent, you should receive the deposit for a booking when your next payment is due from them. For example, an agent who pays their client monthly and receives a deposit for a booking in June should in theory be paying their client this deposit in July. This will of course depend on the date the booking was taken and the date the monthly statements are prepared. Large agencies often charge low or reduced deposits. This is because they know that people are encouraged to book when a small deposit is needed and, in the event of a cancellation, they usually have the means of re-letting the property at short notice. In the event of a booking being cancelled whereby a reduced deposit has been charged, the customer will be expected to pay the remainder of the deposit despite having cancelled their holiday.

The final monies due should be requested *before* the customer takes their holiday. *Never* allow guests to holiday in your property before paying the rental. Although this may seem like common sense, some people can be too trusting and allow guests to sample the property first. This is not to say that your guests are going to be disappointed and therefore refuse to pay, as this is most definitely not what you should be aiming for. If you follow the guidelines set out in this book you should be hoping for repeat bookings, not unhappy guests. However, many people are unwilling to pay for something *after* they have had it and, even if they do pay, you may have to chase your money up and still end up waiting many months for the cheque. All agencies will set a deadline for the balance of the monies to be paid and this can be anything from one to two months in advance. If a booking is taken less than four weeks before the start of the holiday, the agency will request the full amount when taking the booking, and this may be something you would like to consider if you are marketing the property yourself.

If you decide to market your property yourself, bear in mind the length of time it may take you to:

a) chase up the balance of the funds when the due date passes.

b) allow for the payment to reach you.

c) re-advertise the property in the event of a holiday being cancelled.

Of course, we can all be forgetful. If a guest who has booked their holiday and paid the deposit fails to deliver the balance of the monies on time, do not automatically assume they are untrustworthy and immediately offer the property for re-letting. A quick telephone call to remind the guest that the payment is due may be all that is needed. Inform them that you will allow them a further week to post the cheque, after which they stand to lose the deposit they have already paid and you will offer the property for re-letting. This is usually all it takes to get the balance owed to you. Of course, the number of weeks you request the balance of the rental prior to the holiday will need to take into account any further time you allow guests to pay up.

Agencies will have their own strategies for collecting the balance of the monies due. Often late payments can incorporate additional fees or the property would have to be re-booked and the initial deposit lost. An agency will of course furnish potential guests with a contract giving all the details for deposits and balances.

If you employ an agent to take care of the bookings for you, it will be impossible for guests to turn up at your property having not paid the full amount of money due as the agent will not give the property's address and directions until they are in receipt of the full rental funds. Important information about the property such as its full address, directions, housekeeper details, where to obtain the key from and, if used, the code for the key safe, will only be sent out once the customer has paid the rental fees in full. If, however, you are marketing the property yourself you may be asked by a potential guest for the address of the property. Avoid giving the full address at all costs and *never* give details of where to obtain the keys until you have received a firm booking and all the rental fees. Of course, it is acceptable to tell potential customers the vicinity of the property but do not give the precise location.

Remember, although the vast majority of the enquiries you receive will be from genuine holiday-makers, you may also fall victim to opportunists looking for empty properties. Never make things easy for them by giving away too much information early on. Of course, even after receiving the rental in full you cannot guarantee that the people holidaying in your property are honest people who will look after your possessions. If you employ a housekeeper, make sure they keep an eye on the property, without interfering or making a nuisance of themselves. Some property owners instruct their housekeepers to make a note of the car's registration number and to check the property immediately after guests have vacated in order to check for damage and breakages.

Some guests may well abuse your accommodation, but in my experience this is far more likely to happen in a long-term let than in a holiday let. You may well command a rental fee in excess of £400 per week in the summer, even for a small property, and it is probably true to say that guests paying this kind of money usually treat their accommodation with respect, though obviously this is not always the case. Apart from the odd spill, dirty footprints, dog hairs and dirty ovens, on the whole my own rental property has been treated well. You must learn to accept that accidents can and will happen. Unless you feel that your property has been badly damaged or wilfully abused, you must take any accidental damage in your stride as this is part and parcel of what should be accepted in a rental property. It is important when letting your property to see it as a business and not as your home. Although it is vital that your property is welcoming and comfortable, avoid furnishing your accommodation with family heirlooms and very expensive furniture, unless of course your rental more than covers any damage that may occur.

It is worth bearing in mind that the location of your property may also be a factor that contributes to the type of holiday-makers you will attract. For example, many landlords consider large groups of teenage boys to be undesirable guests due to their tendency to want to throw parties and consume alcohol. It is probably true to say that groups of teenagers are more likely to book a holiday in a lively resort where entertainment is on hand. If your holiday home is in the remote highlands of Scotland, this is probably a problem that you will never encounter. You may prefer to rent your property to couples and families, although this is not something that will be easy to monitor. It may be worth considering how you will deal with an enquiry from a teenager, what questions you will ask and whether you will allow them to book. How, in fact, will you be able to tell the age of prospective holiday-makers from their voice on the telephone? You could consider charging a bond, which you will refund should the property be kept in good condition, but of course you risk losing customers if you choose this method.

Cancellations

This can be a tricky one, as usually people do not cancel a holiday unless they really have to. An agent will have a strategy in place for cancellations and will not be deterred by sob stories or personal misfortune which should, in the case of genuine circumstances, be covered by the prospective holiday-makers' insurance policy, if they have one. However, if you are responsible for the bookings yourself, you may well find yourself faced with a dilemma if a holiday-maker telephones you to cancel two weeks prior to their holiday, with a personal tragedy to tell as to why they can no longer go on their holiday. Think about how you would deal with this kind of situation. If an elderly lady requested to cancel her holiday stating that her husband had been taken into hospital, how would you deal with her request for the £500 rental fee she had paid to you to be refunded? You may feel sorry for the lady and her circumstances, but you must also bear in mind that you are running a business and the chances of you being able to re-let your property at such late notice are drastically reduced. Think about whether:

a) you would refund the full amount.

b) you would refund the full amount minus the deposit.

c) you would refund a percentage of the amount.

d) you would not refund anything.

e) you would agree to refund some or all of the money providing you are able to re-let your property.

In theory, you would be well within your rights to keep a percentage of the full amount of money paid as you may not be able to re-let your property; but are you the type of person who would stick to this arrangement? If you refuse to refund any of the money and then end up re-letting your property, you could stand to make twice as much profit, but this appears hardhearted and unfair when someone has had to cancel through difficult circumstances. It is therefore probably reasonable to tell the customer that you would consider refunding their costs only if you are able to re-let your property.

Although some of the people who cancel are doing so for genuine reasons, you may also come across those who have had a change of heart and are relying on your good nature to refund their money should they choose to cancel. This does not make good business sense. If you employ an agent they may well follow a strategy such as the one set out below, and you should bear this in mind when running your own holiday lets:

No. of days before arrival date	Amount payable
More than 56 days	Full deposit
29–56 days	50 per cent of cost of holiday
15–28 days	75 per cent of cost of holiday
1–14 days	90 per cent of cost of holiday
On arrival date or later	Total cost of holiday

There are certain circumstances that will enable guests to qualify for a refund on their insurance policy when cancelling a holiday, such as:

Death (member of the holiday party or a close relative)

Illness

Pregnancy

Redundancy

Jury or witness service

Unable to reach the destination due to an accident en route

Unable to reach the destination due to flooding or heavy snowfall

Different agencies will have differing cancellation circumstances and all guests booking a holiday will be furnished with these conditions.

There may be circumstances when a holiday has to be cancelled by you, the owner, for example in the event of a fire, flood or burglary, and you should have a strategy in place for compensating guests should this unfortunate matter arise. An agency will be in the enviable position of being able to offer alternative accommodation but, unless you have a large property portfolio, you will not be able to offer this service if you are letting your property yourself. You must bear in mind that potential holiday-makers will be disappointed if their holiday is cancelled, particularly at short notice, and you will need to offer acceptable compensation in addition to a full refund. Situations such as these, though hopefully few and far between, must be handled sensitively in order to minimise the disappointment and hopefully reduce the chance of losing potential customers. As an incentive to re-book, should you have to cancel a guest's holiday, consider refunding the monies paid together with an additional amount of money as a goodwill gesture, or perhaps offer the accommodation at a later date at a reduced rate. This will ensure that you retain the booking and therefore hopefully secure another happy customer.

It is because holiday-makers sometimes cancel their bookings that most agencies offer cancellation insurance as part of their package. Some agencies will insist that guests take out their insurance while others will simply recommend it. Agencies usually offer cancellation insurance in scales according to the total value of the holiday booked. If you do not employ an agency to let your property on your behalf, it may be worth doing your own research into holiday cancellation insurance so that you can recommend an insurance company, should your guests require it.

How many bookings can I expect?

As mentioned previously in this book, the number of bookings you can expect will depend on a number of factors, namely:

1. The location of the property.
2. The type of property.
3. The number of guests the property can accommodate.
4. The price.
5. The inclusion of linen, gas and electricity in the rental.
6. The number of attractive facilities, such as an automatic washing machine, dishwasher or cable television.
7. The number of special features, such as a swimming pool, gym or four-poster beds.
8. Whether or not the property accommodates children.
9. Whether or not the property welcomes pets.

Earlier in the book, we talked about the added luxuries you could incorporate when furnishing your property, such as the provision of toiletries or a welcome pack, but these items are not usually advertised and it is therefore the actual facilities on offer that attract potential guests. The items they find on arrival, such as fresh flowers or a bottle of wine, are an added bonus and may well encourage guests to re-book, but they will not be the deciding factors that actually secure a booking.

Most agencies will give you an indication as to the number of bookings an *average* property can expect, but

> Whether you use the services of an agent or let the property yourself, you should be aiming for maximum occupancy and the longest possible season in order to make a good rental income.

these are simply a guideline and must not be taken as gospel. An attractive property in a good location can probably expect to achieve 40 bookings per annum, if it is marketed well. A premier property offering spacious accommodation and luxury amenities such as a swimming pool and a gym may well exceed this number of bookings. Likewise, a character cottage in a romantic setting featuring a four-poster bed may achieve a high number of bookings. Few agents will guarantee a number of bookings and may well inform you that the average properties are reaching between 20 and 30 bookings per annum. If you take into account that many properties only attract visitors during the summer months, this is quite impressive.

It is up to you to ensure that your property has the 'wow' factor and offers prospective guests that little bit more so that they are encouraged to book your property rather than one of the thousands of other self-catering properties on offer.

How can I increase my bookings?

The methods you choose to try to increase your bookings will depend on whether you employ an agent or not. If you are unhappy with the number of bookings you are achieving and you are using the services of an agent, then it is important that you talk to them about your concerns. Ask them why they think you are underachieving and what advice they have to offer to improve your bookings. Many agents share customer feedback with the property owners and by discussing your bookings or lack of them with your agent you may well be able to decide on a plan to help promote your property and encourage people to book. If you are going to ask for advice though, it is important that you heed it, and take on board what the agent is telling you, even if it will entail more work and expense on your behalf. If you have refused to allow pets or smokers into your property in the past, try lifting this ban for the time being and see if it helps to generate more bookings.

> If your agent offers suggestions to improve your property's rental potential, it is important that you heed their advice.

Placing a visitor's book in your property may also open your eyes to problems you did not know existed. Often disgruntled guests who do not wish to lodge a formal complaint with the owner or agency may well let off steam in the visitor's book. Consider yourself lucky if they channel their frustrations in this way, rather than putting their complaint in writing, to either yourself or your agent, but also take on board their criticism. You may have escaped a written complaint, which could warrant a refund, but you will have lost a customer. Take note of their grievances and correct the problem wherever possible.

If you market the property yourself, you will be able to try many different ways of generating more bookings without the restrictions an agent may impose. For example, during a quiet period you may like to consider:

1. Offering friends or family a discount during the quieter weeks.
2. Offering friends or family incentives to help promote your property.

3. Advertising discounts through the winter months.

4. Offering weekend breaks, midweek breaks and short breaks (although always make sure that the price you charge covers the fuel and cleaning bills you will incorporate).

5. Offering any friends who are tradesmen a free or discounted week in return for work done on the property, for example painting and decorating. (Although in theory you will probably only cover your own costs, fuel and cleaning, you will save yourself money by not having to employ a decorator.)

6. Increasing your advertising if there are any special events going on in the area where you have your property. For example, a holiday home near to a watersports club that has competitions for water-skiing or surfing. Find out, in advance, about any forthcoming events and advertise your property in time to incorporate them. Traditional shows, celebrations, Christmas markets and harvest festivals can all attract potential holiday-makers.

Shorts breaks and discounts

If you decide to market your property with an agent, they will ask about your opinion of short breaks. Although they will probably insist that your property is available through-out the year, they do not usually insist that you agree to anything less than a full week's rental. Most agents do, however, offer weekend and short breaks and it is entirely up to you whether or not you are willing to allow your property to be rented in this way. Before agreeing to allow your agent to advertise your property for weekend and short breaks, consider the following:

1. Will the income you receive, after your agent has taken their commission, cover the cost of cleaning the property?

2. Will the income you receive, after your agent has taken their commission, cover the cost of the gas and electricity your guests will use, particularly during the winter months when they are more likely to have the heating on all the time?

3. Is your housekeeper/cleaner available to clean on a Sunday after weekend visitors or midweek after guests who have booked a short break?

4. What is your opinion of short breaks that may be split between two weeks? These have the potential of reducing your income if, for instance, a four-day break is taken in the middle of a two-week period. For example, if your changeover day is usually Saturday, how would you handle a request for a four-day break from Friday to Tuesday? This booking may be welcome if you have no other bookings, but you may well end up turning down two full weeks' lets at a later date.

A good agent will be able to advise you as to the market potential of your particular property. Some properties fair better than others for weekend and short-term lettings. Indeed, some properties such as city flats may make the majority of their income from weekend and short breaks, as guests will book for shopping trips, shows, sightseeing, special events, etc.

If you do not use an agent, you stand to make more money from letting your property for weekends and short breaks as the only expenditure you will have will be the cleaning and fuel costs and there will be no commission fees to pay. However, you must still think carefully about two- and three-day breaks as these may not be profitable. If you are intending to let your property for short breaks, consider a minimum of four days to ensure that the rental you receive will cover the full cost of the expenses you have incurred.

CHAPTER 7 MAINTENANCE

Maintaining the property yourself

Cleaning and maintaining the property yourself will only be a feasible option if you live locally. Be realistic about the distance between your own home and that of your holiday let, and consider how much spare time you have available. There is little point in trying to do all the maintenance and cleaning yourself, just to save a few pounds, if you are running yourself ragged doing so, and cutting corners with regard to the service you are providing.

In my opinion, it is not a good idea to try to clean and maintain the property if it is not within easy reach of your home. Think about how you would get to the property in the middle of winter when there is snow on the ground. You may well have numerous bookings at this time of year, but if you can't get to the property to prepare it for guests, there is little point in trying to secure these bookings.

If you are intending to clean the property yourself, you should choose the changeover day to suit your own personal circumstances. There is no point in taking Saturday to Saturday bookings if you are not available to clean the property and change the bedding on this day. However, bear in mind that the changeover day you choose must also appeal to holiday-makers. Wednesday may be a good day for you to clean the property, but is it realistic to expect guests to plan their holiday to start in the middle of the week? Friday, Saturday and Sunday are the most popular days for holiday let changeovers.

Being on hand to clean and maintain the property personally can have both advantages and disadvantages, and you must weigh each of these up before making your decision.

Advantages of maintaining the property yourself

1. You can be sure that the cleaning is done to a high standard.

2. You save the cost of employing a housekeeper.

3. You can be sure that the property is aired properly.

4. You are on hand to notice any damage, breakages or missing items.

5. You are on hand to give a personal welcome to your guests on their arrival.

6. You are available to sort out any problems personally.

7. You can assess the rate of wear and tear in the property.

8. You can keep a personal eye on your investment and decide whether improvements or cutbacks should be made.

Disadvantages of maintaining the property yourself

1. You will be tied to cleaning on changeover days when you have bookings.

2. You will have the problem of finding someone to stand in for you should you be ill or on holiday.

3. You may be upset at how some people leave your property, particularly if you have emotional ties to the house.

4. Cleaning a holiday let on a regular basis, in addition to working full time, can be exhausting and leave little time for leisure activities.

5. Often the time spent, and the money incurred travelling to the property, can outweigh any money saved by not employing a housekeeper.

6. You may be pestered by holiday-makers encroaching on your time for trivial things.

Regardless of whether you decide to clean the property yourself or employ a housekeeper to do it for you, the property must be spotless at all times. There is no excuse for guests to arrive at a dirty house. Rest assured that they *will* complain if they do not find the property to their satisfaction.

Employing the services of a housekeeper

If you choose to place your property in the hands of a reputable letting agency, they may well be able to assist you with the cleaning and maintenance of your property. Many large, established agencies operate their own cleaning and caretaking service and, although not compulsory, they can be invaluable for the odd clean, perhaps when you or your housekeeper are ill or away on holiday or if you have simply been let down.

Although agency cleaning and caretaking services are helpful in emergencies, it may not be advisable to employ them all the time as they are usually much more expensive than employing a personal cleaner or housekeeper. Depending on the size and location of your property, it is usually more cost-effective to take the time to source a personal housekeeper for the property yourself. Using the agency services will of course guarantee reliability, as they have many employees, but they can often cost twice as much as a personal housekeeper.

If you do not intend to clean the property yourself nor want the trouble of finding your own housekeeper, check that the agency you choose actually has a cleaning and caretaking service, as not all agencies offer this service.

Advantages of using an agency cleaning service

1. Reliable staff who are experienced in cleaning holiday lets.

2. No need to cater for employee holidays and illness, as the agency will have numerous cleaning staff on their books.

3. A high standard of cleanliness should be achieved.

Disadvantages of using an agency cleaning service

1. You will have little say as to the way your property is cleaned and prepared for guests, as most agencies will have their own policies and procedures which they will expect their staff to follow.

2. The service will be impersonal.

3. The service can prove very expensive if used regularly.

4. You may get different staff cleaning your property, making it hard to establish a good, regular routine.

In my experience the best method by far, if you are not able to clean the property yourself, is to employ the services of a personal housekeeper. Admittedly in the first instance you will incorporate a little more work in finding the right person but, when you have done this, the rewards will be worth the effort.

Firstly, you must decide what kind of staff your property will require. If you have a small yard or patio garden, there is little point in paying out for the services of a gardener. If, however, one of the features of your property is a large, well-maintained garden, it is vital that you enlist the help of a gardener, if you are unable to do the gardening yourself. Lawns need mowing at least once a week, sometimes more in the summer months, if they are to remain looking good and to prevent them from turning into a jungle overnight.

When deciding who to employ to clean and maintain your property it is best to use the services of someone who is local. You will hopefully manage to find someone in the same village but, if not, make sure they live in close proximity to your property.

The best way of finding the right person is to advertise for the staff you require. If you are well known in the area where you have your property, and you have managed to make friends already, then you may be able to find a housekeeper simply by asking around. If, however, as in many cases, you do not know lots of people, you would be advised to place an advert in the local newspaper under the heading 'situations vacant' or perhaps put a card in the window of the local newsagents or post office. Newspaper adverts are usually the fastest way of generating interest and can reach a wide audience. Keep your advert short; this will save you money, as you will be charged for the lineage. Something along the lines of the following will suffice:

HOUSEKEEPER REQUIRED

For holiday home in [state area]

Saturday changeovers

Good rates of pay

For more details please contact

[your name and telephone number]

Never put the address of the property in the advert and do not give out too much information. There is no need to advertise how much you are offering to pay, as this can be negotiated if the right person is interested.

It is probably a good idea to place the advert in the local paper a couple of times in order to generate enough interest. Make a list of the people who reply to your advert and set a date, at the holiday property, to conduct your interviews. I cannot stress how important it is to carry out interviews before employing anyone. It may be a bind having to travel to the property and perhaps giving up a day or two of your time to conduct your interviews, particularly if you have quite a distance to travel. However, remember that not only are you trusting this person with the keys to your property, you are also placing the responsibility of keeping your guests happy firmly on their shoulders. Quite often people can sound ideal over the telephone but when you meet them in person they are simply not what you expected. The person you choose as your housekeeper not only has to be a brilliant cleaner with high personal standards, they must also be fit and able to clean a house from top to bottom and to a high standard in a limited number of hours. In addition to being a competent cleaner, they must also be pleasant, polite and approachable as they will probably be the person greeting your guests.

When making a list of the people you are looking to interview, try to ask a few questions while they are on the telephone so that neither you nor they are wasting each other's time. Inform them of your changeover days, so that they can immediately tell you if this is acceptable to them. Even if you state this in your advertisement, people may still apply in the hope of changing your mind or because they intend to fit the cleaning around existing commitments. This is not a good idea. Avoid at all costs employing someone who already cleans a property on the same day as you are intending to do your own changeovers. An experienced housekeeper would not contemplate cleaning two properties on the same day, as they know only too well how much work is involved. If you are expecting to employ someone from 10am until 3pm, it will be impossible for them to be at two properties on the same day. If your changeover day is Saturday and the person answering the advertisement already works on that day, there is little point making an appointment to meet them.

If possible, ask potential housekeepers to bring along a reference and a CV to the interview. Make your appointments with a gap of approximately 30 minutes between. Some people may turn up late, even though this is not how to make a good impression. You will be surprised how quickly the 30 minutes passes, particularly if you have a lot of questions to ask. Avoid showing *everyone* you interview around your property. Instead, tell each potential housekeeper that you are interviewing several people and, should you choose to employ them, you will request that they return at a later time or date so that you can show them the ropes and explain in detail what is expected of them.

Have a list of questions prepared to ask the people you are interviewing, such as:

1. Have they any cleaning experience? If they haven't, make sure they are aware of what will be expected of them. Running around in an apron brandishing a feather duster does not constitute a thorough clean of a holiday home!

2. Are they already working and, if so, where and when do they work?

3. Have they any references? If so, contact them before making your decision.

4. Have they got any holidays booked in the near future? (Although this should not deter you from employing someone you think is suitable, you can at least be prepared to find cover for the dates they are away.)

5. When is the earliest date they can start, should they be offered the position?

You will invariably be asked how much you are willing to pay, but avoid employing anyone who asks this question immediately, even before the job has been outlined. Holiday let cleans can sometimes be seen as 'easy money'. Prospective employees may assume that, because the owner may live some distance away, they will not be on hand to check the work, and they will therefore be able to get away with the bare minimum. This is simply not the case as, even if you cannot see a housekeeper's shabby work, guests certainly will and a dirty property will not be tolerated. It is often not enough to clean a property well – it has simply to be cleaned to perfection!

The number of housekeepers you have to choose from will, of course, depend on the number of replies your advertisement attracts. You may be, as I was, inundated with replies, in which case you will be spoilt for choice, or you may have only one or two replies, in which case you may feel you are picking the best from a bad bunch. Never feel pressurised into employing someone just because there is no other choice. If you do not feel that the person is right for the job, avoid making a mistake. Place another advert in the paper and, in the meantime, consider using the services of your agency or clean the property yourself. Delaying a decision of who to employ as your housekeeper may cause you a little inconvenience and expense but, in the long run, it will be better than employing someone who is simply not up to the job, as you will then have the added problem of having to dispense with their services, re-advertise and conduct more interviews.

If you have plenty of choice, try to select about 10 to 15 hopefuls to interview. Be honest and inform any other candidates that you have been inundated with replies and that you have sufficient people to interview. It is a good idea to take their details and tell them that, should the people you are initially interviewing not be suitable, you will telephone them to discuss the position further. If the worst comes to the worst and you do not find anyone suitable, you then have the added bonus of being able to go back to the other candidates, rather than having to re-advertise.

You may think that a cleaner does not have to be a mastermind and that the job is menial. However, thinking along these lines could seriously damage your holiday let business. Your housekeeper is *the* single most important person. They are the key to the success of your property and whether or not your guests return. It will be their responsibility to impress your guests, to ensure that the property is welcoming and spotless on their arrival and that any problems are dealt with professionally and efficiently.

Things to look for when interviewing potential housekeepers

1. **Friendliness** Your housekeeper must be friendly, polite and approachable.

2. **Professional and efficient** If you are employing the services of a housekeeper, it is probably true to say that you will not be on hand to oversee the cleaning yourself, in which case the person you employ must be able to work under their own initiative. They must be reliable and helpful.

3. **Experienced** You may not need a degree to clean a house. However, you do need to be experienced in cleaning. There is a need for routine, speed and efficiency. There will be a limited number of hours available to clean a property on changeover days and your housekeeper must be able to clean the entire house, thoroughly, during this time. The property may have a stained carpet or broken appliance and it is vital that the person you employ knows how to deal with these extra tasks or potential disasters without panicking.

4. **Smart appearance** The person you employ should appear smart and well turned out. Interviews are primarily for this reason and therefore potential candidates should have made an effort. I am not suggesting that they turn up for an interview in a suit, high heels and carrying a briefcase containing their references, but I would expect to see someone who has pride in their appearance and above all looks *clean*.

Setting the wages you are offering to a potential housekeeper can sometimes be difficult, particularly if you live some distance from the property and are unaware of the going rate for the area. Where some people may think that £10 per hour is fantastic, others may baulk at the suggestion. If there are other holiday lets in your area, try to find out how much they are paying their housekeepers. Enquire how much local cleaners are being paid (bear in mind that there is usually more responsibility involved for a holiday let housekeeper working under their own initiative than, say, a pub cleaner, and you must ensure your wages reflect this). It is also a good idea to enquire how much holiday let agencies in the area would charge for their cleaning services. Some agencies may charge as much as £80 per changeover for their caretaking service, depending on the size of the property, when it may be possible to employ a housekeeper for half that cost.

When you have conducted your interviews, you will hopefully have whittled your choice down to three potential employees. Never set your heart on one person and completely disregard the rest. Bear in mind that a potential candidate may well turn down the job, even if it is offered to them. They may not like the work it entails, the hours or the pay. Try to be flexible and negotiate wherever possible to secure the right person for the job, without compromising too much on what you actually need.

If possible, try to contact the person who is your first choice of housekeeper the same day and ask if they could call on you again so that you can show them around the property and go through the exact requirements of the job. At this second interview, reiterate what the job entails and confirm the wages you are prepared to pay. Try not to give too many instructions all at once or baffle your new housekeeper with details of how to use every piece of equipment. Instead, make a list of the important things they will need to know from day one and, if at all possible, put these in writing so that they can read them at leisure. Suggest that they return to the property on their own, prior to the first changeover, to familiarise themself with the layout of the property and how things work.

This is when you have to be sure that you have taken on the right person for the job and that you have ensured, wherever possible, that they are trustworthy, as you will now be handing over a set of keys to this relative stranger and be expecting them to work under their own initiative and to a high standard. It is important, particularly in the first few weeks of employing a housekeeper, that you ensure that they are doing the job to your satisfaction. The only way you can guarantee this is to visit the property regularly until you are satisfied with their work. Remember that, although you do not want to appear ruthless and demanding, you are paying for a service and you have every right to expect a decent standard. If you are not happy with the way your housekeeper is doing their job, then tell them. Avoid being aggressive, but let it be known that you have some reservations and that you would like some changes to be made.

Advantages of employing a personal housekeeper

1. You will build up a good relationship with the person working for you.

2. You will be able to specify your requirements and know that these will be adhered to, as the same person will be cleaning your property every week.

3. You will probably feel happier leaving the property in the hands of someone you know and trust.

4. You will be able to employ a regular housekeeper at a more reasonable rate of pay than using an agency housekeeping service on a long-term basis.

Disadvantages of employing a housekeeper

1. You may have misjudged the person you interviewed and they may not turn out to be suitable for the job.

2. They may not listen to your requests.

3. They may start off well but later become less enthusiastic and let standards slip.

If you advertise and interview for a housekeeper, you should be able to choose the right person for the job. It is important that the person you employ not only knows how to clean to a very high standard, but that they must also be someone who guests will feel able to approach and, most importantly, someone who *you* can relate to. You need to know that if something is not up to standard, you will be able to tell them and that you can expect them to make the necessary changes.

If you choose well, you should end up with a housekeeper who will hopefully remain in your employment for many years and provide you with a high standard of housekeeping. With the right housekeeper there should be very few disadvantages. However, you should think about:

1. How you will clean your property if your housekeeper is ill.

2. How you will clean your property if your housekeeper is away on holiday.

3. How you will deal with any problems, with regard to the service they are providing you with, should they arise.

Employing the services of a gardener

If your property has a decent-sized garden or if the garden area is a major feature of the property, it is paramount that you employ the services of a gardener, unless you are personally on hand to maintain the garden yourself. Do not underestimate the time needed to maintain a garden to a decent standard. Even a small patio with planted tubs will incur time to sweep, weed and water. A large garden, with flowerbeds and lawns, can be very time-consuming. Guests will be unimpressed if they turn up at a property which it has been stated in the advert has a large family garden, and this turns out to be an overgrown wilderness with garden chairs buried under six feet of grass.

If you live near to your property and the garden is of a manageable size, you may consider taking on the work yourself. However, if you are also intending to do the cleaning of the property, make sure that you have sufficient time between changeovers to carry out all the work to a high standard. If you haven't, consider delegating some of the jobs. Personally I would prefer to employ a gardener as, once established, a garden will only need to be kept tidy and the lawns cut. There should be no major decisions to be made. The house, on the other hand, needs to be immaculate, and personal touches can make all the difference. If you are considering doing some of the work yourself, either to cut down on costs or simply because you have the time and inclination to do so, then I would advise you to take on the housekeeping duties yourself and leave the gardening to a gardener or handyman. Depending on the size of the garden you may get away with employing a gardener for just a couple of hours a week, whereas cleaning an entire house and doing the laundry will take much longer.

If you have a small garden, try to make things easier for yourself by avoiding the temptation to fill lots of tubs with plants. Although these can be very pleasing to the eye they also create a lot of work and, if not watered regularly, will quickly die off in the summer months. There are plants that need little watering which can be very attractive and you should consider these varieties if possible. Paved areas and patios should be kept weed-free and garden furniture should always be in a good, clean state of repair.

Consider providing a barbecue or chiminea for your guests' enjoyment. They can be purchased relatively cheaply and they will enhance the facilities on offer.

Changeovers and cleaning

You will by now have probably already decided on which day of the week to have your 'changeover'. This is the day that a holiday starts and finishes; the day when guests arrive and leave. You should think carefully about the day you choose for your changeovers. Consider:

1. Which day is convenient for you to travel to the property? If you work full time and choose Friday as your changeover day, it will be difficult for you to get to the property to check on the housekeeping service or carry out any routine maintenance, as guests may have already settled in before you arrive.

2. Which is the preferred day for holiday-makers? Saturday seems to be the most popular changeover day by far. Choosing a different day may alienate potential holiday-makers.

3. Saturday changeovers make weekend bookings difficult. Friday changeovers may be a better option if you are intending to let your property for weekends on a regular basis.

4. Which day is the best for the staff you are intending to employ? Your preferred housekeeper may already work during the week and therefore a Saturday or Sunday may be the only days she is available. Try not to compromise too much on the most suitable day for changeovers. Always bear in mind that your guests' preferences are what will secure maximum bookings and this should take precedence over everything else. Aim to find a housekeeper who is willing to fit around the most suitable changeover day for your property and guests.

Whichever day you choose as your changeover day, and whether you choose to clean the property yourself or employ the services of a housekeeper, one thing is paramount – the property must be spotless. Guests are more likely to notice the cleanliness of a property, or lack of it, than anything else. If you have advertised the property as it is and have not overelaborated on its location and facilities, then guests will pretty much be getting what they expect. The cleanliness of the property is therefore the one thing that can make or break a holiday.

Dirty fridges, sticky food cupboards, cobwebs, hairs in the plugholes and mirrors with smudges are a complete put-off. People renting a holiday property expect high standards of cleanliness and it is up to you and your housekeeper to make sure that you do not disappoint. If you can't be on hand to inspect the property after every clean, you should at least make sure that your housekeeper knows exactly what you expect from them. Guests will be quick to complain if a property falls below their expectations of cleanliness.

There may be times when the property looks as if no one has stayed in it, as some guests will clean up after themselves; however, a thorough clean should still be done and skimping on the cleaning routine should be avoided at all costs. You may get a booking for two people in a property which sleeps six and in this case you would expect that most of the beds have not been slept in. However don't be fooled, as this is not always the case. Two people can still use several beds if they have a mind to and can create just as much mess as a family of six. Check all the beds and if you are in any doubt as to whether they have been slept in, play it safe and change them all.

Never underestimate the importance of having a cleaning routine for your holiday cottage. If you employ an experienced housekeeper they will probably have their own routine for cleaning and it is best to let them stick to this providing, when you check the property, it meets with your satisfaction. If, however, you are intending to clean the property yourself, it is a good idea to sit down with a note pad and work out a suitable system that you could use every week on changeover days. By planning, in advance, the jobs that will need doing and the things that are likely to need checking, you will be efficient and avoid the risk of forgetting something important. Your routine will get better with time. Experience is invaluable and like anything, practise makes perfect. The more changeovers you do, the quicker and easier they will become. You will learn which methods work effectively and which system suits you.

It is probably true to say that, if you are thinking of renting out a holiday property, you will already have your own home. If this is the case, you should be familiar with cleaning a house. You will probably already have a routine of your own and many ideas of how you will tackle cleaning your holiday property. However, one very important thing to remember with your holiday let is that you have a very limited timescale to work to. If you are cleaning your own property you probably won't have a deadline to work to, and if you don't get time to do something it is not a big deal as you can postpone it until later. With a holiday let, however, this is not the case. You cannot put off cleaning the oven because you have run out of time! The maximum amount of time between changeovers is usually five hours. Guests may well be requested to leave by 10am and new arrivals will be informed that the property will be ready for them at 3pm. In this time you will have to completely blitz the property. New guests arriving should see no trace of the people who have just left, and the house must be aired, spotlessly clean and welcoming. This is a lot to achieve in just five hours.

The method you choose for cleaning your property will, of course, depend on the layout. My own particular property is spread over three floors, with bedrooms on the top and ground floors and the living space on the first floor. I would always recommend that you start cleaning from the top of the house and work your way down. With a more conventional property, this will mean starting with the bedrooms and family bathroom and ending with the living room and kitchen. Bungalows, of course, are all on the same level, unless they have dormers, but once again I would recommend starting with the bedrooms. One of the first jobs I would recommend you do is to strip off the beds. This will allow them to air while you carry out the other initial tasks before making them up with clean sheets.

Before we look at a tried and tested method for cleaning a holiday property, it is important to go through the kind of cleaning equipment you will need. Always make sure that you have a good supply of cleaning agents, dusters, cloths, etc. at the property and, even if you are cleaning the house yourself, leave the equipment in a locked cupboard at the actual holiday house. If you have to keep loading and unloading your car with the necessary equipment, you run the risk of forgetting something important and wasting precious time.

Your equipment should be kept in a cupboard with a lock to avoid the risk of small children being able to reach it. Invest in some robust, stacking, plastic crates to keep all your equipment handy and accessible. Most hardware stores and supermarkets stock these types of boxes in a variety of colours and sizes. You may like to colour co-ordinate your boxes to make it easier for you to find things. For example, all kitchen cleaning equipment could be in a blue box, while bathroom equipment is in a red box. Similarly, if you purchase larger coloured crates for bedding and towels, you can put all the hand towels in one crate and the bath towels in another. By doing this with your bedding as well, you eliminate the need for wasting time sifting through piles of bedding looking for the correct sheets for the correct bed. Anything that will save time is worth considering.

Keep a box of essentials with you at all times as you go from one room to the next. This will save you having to go backwards and forwards for cleaning materials. Use a robust crate to carry your essential items such as cloths, duster, furniture polish, rubber gloves, bathroom cleaner, disinfectant, toilet cleaner, kitchen cleaner, etc. or, better still, have two boxes, one for the equipment you will need to clean upstairs and the other containing the equipment you will need to clean downstairs. You can replenish your stocks as necessary from the larger boxes you have in your cupboard. Try to keep a good stock of equipment for cleaning, so that you do not have to waste valuable time on the day of the changeover going to the shops to buy things you have run out of. Also, village shops will be more expensive and it will be better for you to purchase your equipment when you go to the supermarket. Bank holidays, Easter and Christmas may also make it difficult for purchasing equipment at the last minute should you run out.

The following is a list of equipment you should always have in stock at your property to use or replace on changeover days:

Dusters	Disinfectant
Dishcloths	Carpet cleaners
Floor cloths	Spare light bulbs
Furniture polish	Toilet rolls
Bathroom cleaners	Bin liners
Shower cleaner	Air fresheners
Kitchen cleaner	Tablets of soap

Mirror/glass/window cleaner

Dishwasher tablets and cleaner or washing-up liquid

Disposable bags for sanitary items and nappies in areas with septic tanks

Soap powder and fabric conditioner

Screwdriver (to tighten up items such as toilet seats which invariably work loose over a period of time)

Replacement food items such as tea, coffee, sugar, salt, pepper, etc.

Spare batteries for remote controls, smoke alarms, etc.

There may well be other items that you may wish to keep at your property, items which you yourself prefer to use. There is a huge amount of cleaning products on the market today and everyone will have their own preferences as to which products they prefer to use. Buy what you consider works well and does the job.

When changeover day arrives, make sure that you get to the property promptly, but not early. If guests are requested to leave by 10am, do not start banging on the door at 9am insisting that they leave. Some guests like to leave early on the last day to avoid traffic in the busy months and because they are aware that the property has to be cleaned and the towels and linen changed in time for the new arrivals. However, there will always be the odd guest who likes to linger. They may even hang around purposefully to let you know how their holiday has been. Pleasant as this may be, it may also eat into the precious time you have to clean the property and you must be diplomatic but firm when getting them to leave. Ideally, when you arrive at the property your guests will already have started their journey home, leaving the house empty for you to begin your cleaning.

The first jobs to tackle are:

1. Open all the windows in the house to eliminate any left-over odours. The house should be free of all cooking, tobacco and dog smells, and the best way to do this is to allow fresh air into the property. Air fresheners are ideal as a last resort, but they only mask odours and their chemicals linger.

2. Strip off all the beds that have been slept in. If the number of guests staying is less than the number the property can accommodate, make sure that you check the other beds. If there is any sign that they may have been slept in, strip these off as well. Put all the dirty laundry in bin liners to take home.

3. Check the oven for spills and burnt offerings. If it is very dirty, spray on the oven cleaner and leave it to work while you tackle the other jobs.

4. Check the carpets and upholstery for spills or marks and if these are major, tackle them as soon as possible in order that they have time to dry out before any new guests arrive.

Now the hard work begins! Starting from the top of the house, work your way around the bedrooms.

Bedrooms

Cleaning the bedrooms:

1. Turn the mattresses on each bed regularly. Turn them both side over side and top to bottom.
2. Bedside rugs should be removed and shook outside.
3. Check the mattress protectors and pillow protectors. If these are stained, change them.
4. Check under the bed for any left items and sweep or vacuum while the beds are stripped off.
5. Polish all furniture, checking the wardrobes and chests of drawers as you go for any items left behind.
6. Dust picture frames and skirting boards.
7. Clean the inside of the window and the sill.
8. Make up the beds with fresh sheets and duvets.
9. Switch on the lights and lamps to check that bulbs do not need changing.
10. Make sure the alarm clock isn't switched on.
11. Draw the curtains to check that they are hanging correctly and have not come off the rail.
12. Wipe paintwork around light switches and door handles.
13. Finally, vacuum the entire room and replace any rugs.
14. Leave a bath towel and hand towel on each bed, along with a small tablet of soap, individual shampoo, bath foam, etc.
15. Arrange any personal items such as cotton wool balls and tissues on the dressing table.

All bedrooms should be cleaned methodically in this way. I would recommend that, in a traditionally laid-out property, you should tackle the bedrooms first, followed by the bathrooms, to avoid having to continually change your cleaning equipment from duster and polish to cloth, mop and disinfectant.

Bathrooms

Next to the kitchen, bathrooms are generally the areas where dirt and grime will accumulate. You can avoid the build-up of water marks and scum by leaving a bathroom cleaner and cloth for your guests to use themselves. Most people will use products that have been provided to help to keep the property clean.

Cleaning the bathrooms and shower rooms:

1. Spray the bath and shower area with a suitable cleaner and wipe around. Treat any stubborn stains more vigorously.

2. Remove any hair from the plug holes in both the bath and hand basin.

3. Wipe down all tiles.

4. Clean mirrors.

5. Clear out cabinets and wipe down with a suitable solution.

6. Clean the toilet. Make sure that you clean both inside and outside the pan and under the seat. Wipe the handle and hinges and pour in a generous amount of toilet cleaner.

7. Clean the wash basin and taps and wipe dry.

8. Clean the inside of the window and the sill.

9. Dispose of any left-over soap, shampoo and bubble bath.

10. Empty the bin and replace with a clean liner.

11. Remove dirty bath and pedestal mats and replace with clean ones.

12. Check light bulbs and replace if necessary.

13. Draw curtains or pull blinds to check for splashes, and wipe where necessary.

14. Replace the toilet roll with a full one.

15. Leave an adequate supply of bags for sanitary items and disposable nappies.

16. Wipe around shaving adapter plug and door handle.

17. Mop the floor with a fresh-smelling disinfectant solution if tiled or linoleum, or vacuum thoroughly if carpeted.

Hall, stairs and landing

Cleaning the hall, stairs and landing is relatively straight-forward. Use a brush or vacuum cleaner to remove fluff and debris. Check light bulbs and replace if necessary. Clean windows and sills and remove any dead flies and cobwebs. Wipe down handrails and around light switches to eliminate grubby finger marks.

Once the bedrooms have been tackled, you can get to work on the kitchen and living areas.

Kitchen

Cleaning the kitchen:

1. Tackle the oven first. If it has been left in a particularly bad state, you should have already added the cleaner so that it can have been working on the grease while you have been busy cleaning the bedrooms and bathrooms. Wipe the oven out and make sure the grill pan and shelves are clean.

2. Wipe down the hob, making sure you remove any stains.

3. Remove all dirty tea towels and oven gloves.

4. Dispose of the dishcloth.

5. Empty all the food cupboards, the fridge and the freezer, and dispose of left-over food. Never leave any food for the next guests, even if it is well within its sell-by date.

6. Empty crumbs from the toaster.

7. Wipe out the food cupboards and concentrate on any sticky surfaces or spilt substances.

8. Wipe out the fridge and freezer and leave the door open for them to air for as long as possible.

9. Empty the bin, wipe down with a disinfectant solution and replace with a fresh liner.

10. Remove all appliances from the work surfaces and wipe these thoroughly with a suitable spray or cream cleaner.

11. Re-arrange the appliances such as the toaster and kettle.

12. Clean the window and the sill.

13. Wipe out the microwave and leave the door open for it to air for as long as possible.

14. Check cupboards containing crockery and glasses for crumbs and breakages, and replace items as necessary.

15. Wipe out the cutlery drawer. This is one area where crumbs invariably gather. Check the cutlery has been washed satisfactorily.

16. Put any items that need another wash into the dishwasher and switch on, or hand wash them in the sink.

17. Check the curtains or blind for splashes and wipe where necessary.

18. Empty the kettle.

19. Clean the sink and taps and wipe over tiled areas.

20. If new guests are arriving that day, place an unopened, fresh pint of milk in the fridge.

21. Arrange a welcome tray containing teabags, coffee, sugar and biscuits.

22. If you provide a grocery pack, place this in the cupboard.

23. Arrange a small vase of fresh flowers on the windowsill or table.

24. Check light bulbs and change if necessary.

25. Wipe around door handles and light switches.

26. Mop the floor with a fresh-smelling disinfectant solution.

27. Leave two clean tea towels, oven gloves and two disposable dishcloths for guests to use. I would recommend the use of disposable dishcloths. They can be thrown away and are much more hygienic than fabric dishcloths, which attract and hold germs and bacteria.

28. It is always a good idea to leave a small selection of cleaning materials under the sink. Dishwasher tablets and an anti-bacterial work surface cleaner will be beneficial.

29. Empty the dishwasher and replace the items in the cupboard.

30. Close the doors on the white goods you have left open, once they have aired.

Utility room

Cleaning the utility room:

1. Make sure the soap powder dispenser of the washing machine is clean and void of any left-over powder that has turned to sludge.
2. Check that previous occupants have not left any clothing in either the washing machine or the tumble dryer.
3. Wipe down the front of both appliances.
4. Clean the filter in the tumble dryer.
5. Wipe the sink and taps.
6. Check the light bulbs and change if necessary.
7. Wipe around the light switch and door handles.
8. Mop or vacuum the floor.

The bathrooms, kitchen and utility room must stand up to close scrutiny. These will be the rooms that most guests will look at closely to judge the cleanliness of the whole house and it is therefore vital that you go the extra mile and make sure that they are completely spotless.

Dining room

This should be relatively easy to clean, providing there are no food spills to tackle. If possible, try to avoid using carpet in high-traffic areas such as halls and dining rooms, as these are the places where carpets become shabby the quickest.

Cleaning the dining room:

1. Tackle any spills on carpets or upholstered chairs with a good-quality cleaner.

2. Polish sideboards, cupboards and the dining table. Make sure that you tackle any left-over food particles on the table and eliminate any traces of previous guests.

3. Clean windows and sills.

4. Draw curtains to check they are still hung well.

5. Check light bulbs and replace if necessary.

6. Dust picture frames and skirting boards.

7. Arrange fresh flowers in a vase and place in the centre of the table.

8. Thoroughly vacuum the carpet.

9. Wipe around door handles and light switches.

Living room

Try to keep knick-knacks to a minimum. You must find a happy medium when decorating and accessorising your holiday property. Too few vases and ornaments will look cold and unwelcoming, too many will be a nightmare to clean and result in breakages. Avoid cramming shelves with lots of clutter, as these are particularly awkward and time-consuming to dust if you have to remove dozens of items first.

Cleaning the living room:

1. Remove all cushions from sofas and armchairs. You may find an assortment of things that have slipped down between the cushions, such as loose change, sweet wrappers or even the remote control for the television. Remove any objects you find and using the attachments on your vacuum cleaner, give the sofa and chairs a thorough clean, removing fluff, hair and crumbs. When you have finished, plump up the cushions and set them back in place.

2. Polish all shelves and surfaces.

3. Dust picture frames and skirting boards.

4. Wipe over the television set and any games consoles to remove dust and finger marks.

5. Take rugs outside and give them a good shake.

6. Clean any windows and sills. Pay particular attention to patio doors as these can attract dogs and young children, who will leave behind a variety of smudges and sticky finger marks.

7. If your property has an open fire, clean this thoroughly and fill the basket with wood and the scuttle with coal for the next guests.

8. Check all light bulbs and change if necessary.

9. Wipe around light switches and door handles.

10. Arrange fresh flowers in a vase.

11. Vacuum the carpet thoroughly, moving furniture where necessary.

12. Check the remote controls, etc. and replace batteries where necessary.

Conservatory

Cleaning the conservatory:

1. Remove cushions from cane furniture and shake well.

2. Using the attachments from your vacuum cleaner, remove any dust and food particles before replacing the cushions.

3. Wipe down any tables and surfaces.

4. Clean windows where necessary.

5. Mop the floor with a solution of fresh-smelling disinfectant.

6. Check light bulbs and replace if necessary.

7. Wipe around light switches and door handles.

There is no room in the house that can be spared a thorough clean. Each room has its own unique purpose and the standard of cleanliness must be high in each one. Although it is probably true to say that most guests will spend the majority of their time in the living room, this is by no means the only room you should really concentrate on. Who would relish cooking in an oven caked in grease or sleeping in a bed with grubby sheets? Every room has its own check points and potential pitfalls to look out for.

Additional jobs to tackle

There are a number of other jobs you will need to do at every changeover, but some of these will depend on the facilities you provide and the guests you are willing to accommodate. For example:

1. If you agree to allow smokers in your property, make sure you empty and wash every ashtray and leave them in easily accessible places.

2. If you allow dogs in your property, wash and dry pet bowls and place them on a clean mat in the area of the house where you would like them to be fed. If you have a conservatory or porch, this is an ideal place to leave the bowls and hopefully your guests will take the hint. It is also a good idea, as I have mentioned before, to leave a couple of clean, old towels for guests to use to dry off their dogs when they have been out walking. It is much easier for you to wash a couple of towels than to scrub floors and carpets to try to eliminate muddy paw prints.

3. Regardless of the type of property you have or who you are willing to accommodate, you must *always* check your smoke alarms before the arrival of new guests. Make sure you test every alarm and replace batteries as and when necessary. It is a good idea to

make a note of when you have changed batteries, in order that you can make sure that your alarms are in good working order at all times.

Some jobs around the house will need doing less frequently. You may be well advised to make a note of these jobs and write next to them the frequency at which they should be done and the date they were last carried out. There may be some weeks when you have no bookings and this would be an ideal time to carry out the less frequent jobs, as you will have more time to spend. However, do not neglect these tasks if you are lucky enough to have endless bookings. Tackle one or two every week, note down what you have done, and see which jobs still need to be done. This way everything will get done in its turn, without things being neglected or duplicated. Some of the less frequent jobs may be:

1. Cleaning the windows. Although any marks on either the inside or outside should be removed at every changeover, a thorough clean of the windows may only need doing once a month. This will depend on the location of your property. Houses on a busy road or near to the coast may need their windows cleaning more often due to traffic pollution or sea salt. Consider employing a window cleaner to give your windows a good clean once a month, particularly if your property has a lot of large or difficult-to-reach windows.

2. Dusting the tops of cupboards and wardrobes. Although it is probably fair to say that dust will accumulate in these places on a weekly basis, you will not have the time to clean them after every changeover. Be honest, do you clean the top of the cupboards and wardrobes in your own home every week? It is highly unlikely that guests will climb up to look at the top of your wardrobes, so this is a job that can be tackled when the time allows. However, bear

in mind that guests may put an empty suitcase or holdall on top of a wardrobe so that it is out of the way during their stay. If you fail to clean regularly, they will notice when they remove their case!

3. If you have a character cottage that is heavily laden with old beams, though they may look beautiful they will invariably provide you with extra work. It is not necessary to dust all the beams at every changeover, although you would be well advised to inspect them and remove any visible cobwebs.

4. Removing books from shelves and dusting behind them. If you only have a few books, this will not be difficult. However, if you have a large collection of books it may be better to tackle this task a little and often, perhaps cleaning several shelves each week.

5. Touching up paintwork.

6. Removing large items of furniture or appliances to vacuum or mop behind. Fridges and washing machines should be pulled out periodically and cleaned behind. So too should chests of drawers and beds.

> Try to keep on top of these jobs by carrying out one or two tasks at every changeover, rather than leaving everything to build up.

You may get away with dusting banisters and picture frames less often, but by using a feather duster with a long handle this is by no means a difficult job and can be done quite easily on each changeover day.

Another point you should consider is how you will go about cleaning a property if it has been booked for two weeks rather than one. It will still be necessary for the bed linen and towels to be changed on a weekly basis. If you employ the services of an agency to market your holiday let for you, you will have no say in how this is done as they will have their own policies. However, if you are cleaning the property yourself or if you employ a personal house-keeper, you would be advised to ask the guests for their own preference on whether or not they require the property to be cleaned midway through their stay. There are pros and cons either way.

Advantages for cleaning midway through a two-week stay

1. It sets a good example and may well impress your guests who are not expecting this kind of service.

2. It will make it easier to clean the property at the end of the stay if some of the dust and dirt is removed after the first week.

3. It is a good opportunity to find out what your guests think about your property and whether they are enjoying their holiday. Granted, this may be when guests who have an axe to grind will take the opportunity to complain, but at least this will give you the chance to put things right and hopefully smooth over any problems.

4. You will be able to take the dirty laundry home with you to wash and iron in time for the next changeover.

Disadvantages for cleaning midway through a two-week stay

1. It may be uncomfortable being in the house when the guests are out. You will be around their personal belongings, some of which may be valuable. It is advisable either to arrange for a time to clean

when the guests are in, or failing this take someone with you.

2. Not all guests will thank you for invading their privacy and they may even suspect you are checking up on them.

3. It will be difficult to carry out a thorough clean as you will be cleaning around guests' possessions.

4. You may not like what you see. Although you will be unable to do a thorough check of the property, particularly if the guests are present, you may well notice damage or a situation that you are not happy with. You need to be able to deal with this kind of situation effectively and amicably.

5. If guests prefer to change their own bedding, you will have to arrange a suitable time with them to collect the dirty laundry. Failing that, you will have double the wash load the following week.

I would advise you to ask your guests, on their arrival, which method they prefer. In my experience, guests have been pleasantly surprised at the offer of a clean midway through the stay and are happy for someone to change the beds and run round with the vacuum cleaner for them – after all, they are on holiday. However, at the other end of the spectrum, some people go away on holiday to be left alone. They may feel they have to tidy up before you arrive or they may simply value their privacy when away on holiday. Respect your guests' wishes. If they request you to come and clean, ask them for a suitable time. Do not barge in at 9am and expect everyone to be up and dressed! If they wish to change the beds themselves, leave them with sufficient bed linen and towels, wish them a pleasant stay and be prepared for a heavy clean on their departure.

If you do employ the services of a housekeeper, I would always recommend that you pay them for two changeovers during a two-week booking, regardless of whether or not guests have requested that they come in and change the beds and clean around for them. The housekeeper may not have to spend time at the property on both weekends, but rest assured they will most definitely earn their money when, the following week, they have twice the amount of dirt and grime to clean and double the laundry to do!

Inspections

If you do not carry out the cleaning of your holiday property yourself, it is paramount that you visit regularly to ensure that whoever you have trusted with the housekeeping is maintaining a good standard and working to your own requirements.

If you have decided to place the cleaning of your property in the hands of a letting agency, do not take it for granted that everything will be perfect. Whoever is looking after your property for you needs to know that you are on hand and that you are available when needed. If you don't take an interest in your own property, why should you expect anyone else to? I am not saying that without you constantly checking up on them, every housekeeper you employ will be lazy and slapdash. However, I am saying that it is in your own interests to keep a close eye on things and make sure the person you employ is working to your own expectations and high standards.

When you first employ a new housekeeper, try to visit the property on changeover days every week for the first three or four weeks. They will feel happier knowing you are there to offer help and assistance and you will feel happier knowing that the job is being done properly. As time goes by and you feel confident about your new employee, you will be able to leave a bigger gap between your visits. It is always a good idea to call at the property unannounced occasionally during the changeover clean. If your housekeeper is doing their job well they will have no objections to you doing this, and if they are not then you will be on hand to sort it out immediately.

CHAPTER 8
RECEIVING GUESTS

ARRIVALS

It is important that guests feel welcome on their arrival at your holiday property. Whether you are on hand to greet them yourself or you employ a housekeeper to do this for you, it is vital that whoever meets your guests is polite, helpful and approachable.

When guests arrive at your property, they may have endured a long and stressful journey, they may have tired, hungry children or they may simply wish to put the kettle on and sit down. Tread carefully when guests first arrive and try not to outstay your welcome. In some cases, it may be best simply to drop off the keys and point them in the direction of the information folder before leaving them to unpack and unwind.

You should be able to gauge the type of holiday guest you have in the first few minutes. If they appear stress-free and happy to chat, you could take the time to point out where things are and how they work. However, some people hate the idea of making polite conversation with a stranger and would prefer to find things out for themselves. If this is the case, hand over the keys and inform them of your contact details in case they need them, and leave them to it.

Always make sure that your guests are aware that they can contact you at any time, should they have a problem or query.

If you are not on hand to welcome your guests personally, you must ensure that you have a fool-proof method for handing out the keys. Your housekeeper may agree to do this for you, but what happens if guests do not arrive until very late at night? It is not very fair to expect your housekeeper to be on call all day and all night just to hand over keys.

I would always recommend that, whenever possible, there is someone present to greet guests personally; however, it is essential that you have a back-up system in case of late arrivals. I have found the use of a good-quality key safe to be the answer. Invest in a key safe with a number combination and place this out of direct view on the property. Do not advertise the fact that there is a key on hand by placing the safe next to the door bell! Even if your property is in a low crime rate area, advertising keys in this way is not a good idea.

If you are letting your property through an agency, inform them of your intentions to use a key safe and let them know the combination number. They will only inform guests of the number when they have paid in full and have already furnished them with the address and directions to the property. If you are letting the property yourself, obviously the same will apply, and you should only inform guests of the combination to the safe after they have paid the full cost of the holiday.

Key safes are a good back-up choice. They prevent guests from having to hang around outside the property, waiting for the arrival of you or your housekeeper, should they arrive earlier than expected, and they avoid the need for guests to have to pick the keys up from your own or your housekeeper's residence. An alternative to a key safe is to ask a neighbour to hold a set of keys for you, but again they will have the same problem as your housekeeper, and you should not expect them to be available to greet your guests at any time of the day or night.

Prior to the guests arriving, always make sure that you have furnished them with accurate directions on how to find your property. There is nothing worse than holiday-makers starting their holiday off on the wrong foot due to complicated directions. Remember, *you* may know the area well, but guests could be travelling from the other end of the country and have no idea where they are going. It is up to you to ensure they do not spend hours looking for your property due to poor directions. If you employ the services of a letting agency, they will furnish guests with directions to the property and instructions for obtaining the keys.

Once your guests have arrived at the property, they will have their own expectations of what they hope to find. It is almost impossible to please *all* of the people *all* of the time, but you must always strive to please *most* of the people *most* of the time. Try to anticipate what guests will expect and, wherever possible, provide it. Ask yourself what you would like from a holiday cottage and try to make the first impression one of a high-standard, well-equipped holiday property.

Guests will invariably expect:

1. Simple, easy-to-understand directions to the property.
2. A fool-proof method of acquiring the keys to the property.
3. A clean, warm and welcoming property.
4. Appliances that are simple to use.
5. Hot water on arrival.

You can impress guests by going that little bit further and providing:

1. A welcome tray with tea, coffee, sugar and milk.
2. Fresh flowers.
3. Toiletries.

I cannot stress strongly enough that the need to ensure that the property is spotlessly clean is the most important thing any owner or housekeeper can do. Added touches, such as a welcome tray, are pleasant and will be well received, but they will never take the place of cleanliness. A bottle of wine or a vase of fresh flowers will not appease guests who find the state of the bathroom unacceptable or the sheets grubby.

What kind of written advice should I leave for guests?

It is important that the information you leave for guests is accurate and straightforward. Try not to bombard them with information that is unnecessary and irrelevant, as pages and pages of instructions and information can be very off-putting. Guests holidaying in your property for a week will not want to spend three days of their time sifting through the folder of information you have left them!

REMEMBER

Too much information in your folder will put guests off reading it, and too little information may result in guests contacting you often for help and advice. Pay special attention to the details you supply and only provide accurate, relevant information.

It is important to remember that most guests will turn to your information folder upon arrival, so it must be well written and informative. Replace any worn, marked or ripped pages and update the information regularly. It is a good idea to have a ring binder with loose pages rather than a book for providing guests with information. This way pages can be added or removed when necessary, without spoiling the overall effect of the folder. I would recommend that you laminate the pages before placing them in the folder. This helps to keep the pages looking clean and fresh all the time and avoids tears and stains which will invariably occur when hundreds of people have thumbed through them.

The information you put in your folder should include:

1. A note from you welcoming the guests to your property and wishing them an enjoyable stay.

2. Your address and contact number, together with that of your housekeeper, if you employ one. If you do not live in close proximity to your property, make sure your information folder clearly states the first point of contact in an emergency or for help and advice. It is always nice to inform your guests of your own details in case they have a problem or complaint which they prefer not to share with anyone except the owner of the property.

3. Emergency telephone numbers and addresses such as the nearest doctor, hospital, police station, dentist and vet.

4. Details of where guests can park and any local restrictions.

5. Any security details for the property, for example details of the alarm system.

6. Simple, easy-to-follow instructions on how to work the heating and hot water systems.

7. Simple, easy-to-follow instructions on how to work the electrical appliances in the property, such as the washing machine, tumble dryer, microwave and oven.

8. Simple, easy-to-follow instructions on how to work any fires or stoves in the property.

9. Details of where to find the stopcock.

10. Details of where to find the fuse box.

11. Details of where to find the fire extinguishers and fire blanket.

12. Details of the refuse collections: when bins should be left out and where to leave them.

13. Details of the nearest rubbish tip and recycling centres.

14. Details of how the television, video, DVD, games consoles, etc. work.

15. Details of any special instructions for the toilet if your property is not on a mains sewerage system or has a septic tank.

Remember, if you do not leave instructions on how to operate equipment, or if your instructions are complicated and difficult to understand, guests will simply play around with the appliances and this often results in damage. It is therefore in everyone's interests to take the time to write down how to operate the equipment and appliances in easy-to-understand terms. If you have them, you may like to leave the manufacturer's guides out as well. In addition to the information file, it is a good idea to photocopy and laminate the instructions for appliances such as the oven and washing machine and display these next to the equipment. Guests will often refer to the instructions when placed in easy view by the appliances, before sifting through a folder of information for the instructions they require. A simple guide pinned up next to the washing machine stating the most popular programmes will be very helpful to guests who have never used your machine before.

Areas that are not served by mains sewerage pipes may well have special instructions which must be followed to prevent blockages. Make sure that, in addition to mentioning these instructions in the information file, you also pin a small notice next to each toilet in the property to jog the minds of guests and to inform those who have not taken the time to read the information in the folder.

Other details that should be mentioned in your information file are:

1. Details of local attractions. Guests will be impressed by any information you can supply them with, and this is your chance to sell your property and its area

to them. If you can encourage guests to explore the local area, they may well be encouraged to return to your property for another holiday, particularly if they have not managed to sample everything on offer during their initial stay.

2. Details of the best beaches in your area. State which beaches allow dogs and which are particularly suitable for families.

3. Provide details of where guests can go fishing, water-skiing or diving, if your property is near the sea.

4. Provide details of the best places to shop for local produce.

5. Inform guests of the best pubs and restaurants in the area, which ones welcome children and which are open all day.

6. Give details of the best walks around the area, and what to avoid.

Any *local* information you can provide for your guests will be very welcome and will help holiday-makers to settle in quickly and feel part of the community. No one likes to feel like an outsider and the more help and advice you make available to guests, the quicker they will adapt to their surroundings and begin to enjoy their holiday.

It is a good idea to provide a visitor's book. These can be purchased for about £10–£15 from bookshops and stationers. If you employ the services of a letting agency such as Country Holidays, they will provide you with a visitor's book initially. Visitor's books enable your guests to record their own findings for the use of others and will give them a way of informing you about the best (and worst) parts of their holiday. Avoid ripping out pages that may not be entirely complimentary. Future guests will immediately notice if the visitor's book has been tampered with and will often jump to the wrong conclusion, imagining the remarks to be much worse than they probably were. Rest assured, if anyone has a serious complaint to make it is highly unlikely that they will do so through the visitor's book.

The personal touch

Your property will be one of many thousands of holiday properties available to rent for holidays each year. Whether you manage and let your property yourself or pay an agency to do this for you, be under no illusions, you will be up against a lot of competition. There are hundreds of thousands of people who, just like you, are hoping to make money from letting their property to holiday-makers. Even if your property is in a small village, it is probably true to say that there will be other houses for let in the area. Whether or not your own property letting will be successful will depend on:

1. How many other properties are available for letting in your chosen area. Competition is fierce. If there are lots of other properties available, do not be too disheartened. If the area is very popular with holiday-makers, the demand will be high and it is still possible that you will be able to let your property for a reasonable number of weeks each year. However, you will have to be extra vigilant and make sure that your property has things to offer that the others do not, in order to secure the maximum number of bookings.

2. The attractions available to holiday-makers. If your chosen area is in a quiet backwater and lacks shops and restaurants, it is essential that you market it at walkers and country lovers looking for a quiet restful holiday in relaxing surroundings. Do not try to lure people there under false pretences – they will not

enjoy their stay and may well complain if the area and the amenities are not what they expected.

3. Think about providing your own additional services to enable holiday-makers to utilise the property and its area to the maximum. If your property is in the heart of the countryside, think about investing in a few bicycles for the guests to use. If your property is part of a farm, allow visitors to look around and perhaps arrange tours for your guests to take part in milking the cows or watching the sheep shearing. Children, in particular, are fascinated by the workings of a farm. If your property is near to the sea, consider investing in a small boat, canoe or dinghy for the pleasure of your guests. (If you are thinking of providing some of these services, it is important to check with your insurance company first to ensure that you are covered for any claims that may arise from them.)

As competition is likely to be high if your property is in a sought-after area and holiday let properties are in abundance, it is essential that you do all you can to ensure that your property stands out from the crowd and generates as many bookings as possible. If your guests have had a good holiday, it is highly probable that they will re-book and tell their friends and family, and this is something that you should be aiming for. Many established holiday lets are visited by the same people year after year and are booked up many months in advance. As a holiday home owner this is something you should be trying to achieve in order to maximise your property's letting potential.

Competition is really only considered valid if the properties available are of a similar size and in the same type of location. Twenty properties within a seaside town will not all be considered potential competitors if ten are situated on the outskirts of the town, four are flats, three are large properties sleeping twelve people and the remainder do not allow pets. Out of the number of properties available near to your own, you should only consider those of a similar size and offering similar facilities to your own as being in direct competition.

If your property is within a small cluster of similar-sized houses on the seafront and several of these are also available to let, you will have your work cut out trying to make sure that your property stands out from the rest. If you market and let the property yourself you could look at the prices the others charge and make yours slightly cheaper. However, you risk alienating yourself from your neighbours by doing this and could be out of pocket if you do not charge what your property is worth.

Holiday-makers, though looking for value for money, will not usually be persuaded to book a less appealing property just to save £10 or £20. Instead of reducing the price, you should be looking to improve the accommodation, and this is where the personal touch can swing it for you. Often guests will not appreciate the personal touches until they arrive at the property. Therefore it is essential to advertise any special features so that potential holiday-makers are aware of the service on offer before they book. Impressing guests on arrival and during their stay is an excellent way of making sure that they enjoy their holiday, and they may well re-book with you and tell friends and family of their good experience, which may result in future bookings.

The personal touch does not necessarily have to cost you anything, though spending a little on luxuries usually pays dividends. Think about things like:

1. Ensuring that guests have a hassle-free journey by providing them with accurate directions of how to find your property.

2. Offering a warm welcome when guests arrive, being polite and approachable.

3. Making sure that the property is clean and well aired.

4. Making sure that, if children are expected, all the necessary safety equipment is available and in a good state of repair.

5. Ensuring that all the appliances and equipment have been checked and are in good working order prior to guests arriving.

6. If you are expecting guests with dogs, provide feeding bowls and towels for them to use.

In addition to the way you present your property to guests, you may also like to think about providing little extras that can make their stay more comfortable and impress them at the same time.

Providing toiletries and food packs

Holiday let accommodation is becoming more and more popular and many people now prefer to go on self-catering holidays rather than stay in a hotel. Guests on self-catering holidays can please themselves where and when they eat and they generally have much more freedom. The demand for high-quality accommodation is huge and guests are beginning to expect more and more from their accommodation. In the days of virtual tours, when potential guests can view the property on line before they book, there is no place for shabby furnishings and pokey houses in run-down areas. In addition to the high standard of accommodation expected, more and more holiday-makers rely on the property owner or letting agency to go that little bit further and provide them with a welcome tray. Of course, not all guests expect this, but if you can anticipate the needs and preferences of most of your guests, and pleasantly surprise the remainder, you will be on to a winner. Providing welcome trays and toiletries need not be expensive and, if you put the cost into perspective against the week's rental, you will see how spending a small amount of money can pay dividends towards customer satisfaction. If one guest is prompted to re-book with you because of the extras you provide, you will have more than made back the money you have spent on extras throughout the entire year's bookings!

What you provide in a welcome tray or pack should depend on the type of property you own and how much you charge for a week's accommodation. No one would expect you to spend £20 on a welcome pack if you are only charging £100 for the week's rental. Not only would this be inappropriate, but you would quickly start to lose money. If you own a small property and are asking around £200–£400 per week in rental, I would advise you to provide extras such as:

1. Tea, coffee, sugar and milk sufficient for the number of guests holidaying at the property. You are only required to leave sufficient for guests to enjoy a hot drink on arrival and should not be leaving tea bags, coffee, etc. to last them the whole week.

2. A packet of decent biscuits or a small cake. If you enjoy baking, these could be homemade. If not, try to buy cakes or biscuits that reflect the local area. For example, delicious ginger biscuits are made in Grasmere, and if your property was near to this area of the Lake District, providing a packet of locally made ginger biscuits would be a nice touch.

3. A bottle of decent wine. This is a particularly welcome addition at Christmas time or if you are aware that your guests are celebrating a special occasion such as

an anniversary or birthday. You will not be expected to splash out on a bottle of champagne, but neither would guests thank you for a bottle of cheap plonk from the local supermarket. If you are intending to leave a bottle of wine, invest in something around the £5 to £6 mark. A cheap bottle is worse than none at all, and will not impress your visitors.

4. Fresh flowers. These need not cost a lot of money, and if your property has a garden, you could even pick them yourself. A small bunch of carnations or chrysanthemums add a pleasing touch and, if the flowers are scented, provide an added bonus.

5. Toiletries. Again, do not go overboard and provide guests with a complete basket of toiletries, but stick to a small bar of individually wrapped guest soap placed with the towels.

If your property is in the higher price band and you are commanding rents in excess of £500-plus per week, you will have the money to provide your guests with a little more luxury:

1. Instead of a welcome tray, consider providing a hamper containing the usual tea, coffee, sugar, milk and biscuits or cake, but with the addition of eggs, bread, milk, jam, cheese, marmalade, orange juice and butter. If your property is on or near a farm, you may also like to provide a selection of seasonal fruit and vegetables.

2. A decent bottle of wine and a box of chocolates would be a nice touch at Christmas or if your guests are celebrating a special occasion.

3. Fresh flowers. A suitable arrangement of fresh flowers would be a nice touch. A bunch of flowers costing around £10 would fill several vases and provide colourful focal points around the property.

4. Toiletries. If you are commanding a higher rental for your property, you may like to supply your guests with a selection of complimentary toiletries. In addition to individually wrapped soaps, you can also purchase small bottles of shampoo, conditioner and bath/shower gel. These can be purchased in bulk and, depending on the number of bookings you receive, should last many months. The companies who supply these goods usually supply hotels and guest houses. Bars of soap can be purchased in bulk in multiples of 500 for around £30, working out at a cost of just 6p each – a small price to pay to impress your guests and provide them with a little luxury.

5. Cotton wool pads and tissues. Placed on the dressing table, these are a useful, inexpensive addition which most guests will appreciate.

6. Bathrobes and slippers. Some of the more upmarket holiday properties may like to provide these. Again, they can be purchased from the same companies that supply your toiletries. However, it is important to remember that bathrobes and slippers will need washing and may even end up in your guest's suitcases!

Christmas bookings

If you have bookings for your property over the Christmas and New Year period, you must spend a little more time preparing the property for your guests. You will be expected to provide a Christmas tree, tastefully decorated, but you may also like to provide a few additional luxuries for your guests. For example, if children will be present, consider wrapping a small selection box for each child. These can be purchased for a couple of pounds and should please both parents and children. A box of mince pies, a Christmas cake, bottle of sherry and some crackers would also be a nice touch. Often guests pay a premium when they are holidaying at Christmas and the New Year and, as it does not actually cost you, the owner, any more than it would if they were holidaying on 25 November, you will have a little extra cash to play about with. Do not go over the top with your provisions, however. You should always be aiming to make a profit and remember, if the guests re-book for July they may expect a similar welcome!

Before planning how to decorate your property for Christmas and the New Year, it is important to remember to check with guests first. Most people will be going on holiday to celebrate Christmas, but some may have reasons for escaping the pressures of this time of year and will not thank you for reminding them of the occasion if this is the case. Similarly, some people do not celebrate Christmas and this is something you should bear in mind when deciding what to provide.

If you have guests travelling late on Christmas Eve, remember that shops will be closed when they arrive and may well stay shut for a few days, so ask your guests if they would like you to provide a grocery pack, for which you should charge them extra. Many people will bring their own groceries with them, but most will welcome the offer of assistance.

Grocery packs

Christmas aside, the offer of providing a grocery pack is a nice touch for all guests. If you live nearby and have the time, it is a good idea to ask guests if they would like you to do a little shopping for them in order that they have the basics available on their arrival. If you do offer this service, ask guests what they would like you to provide and make sure they are aware that they will be expected to pay for the groceries. It is essential that you ask how much they are prepared to spend and provide them with a receipt for the goods. Ideally you will be paid for any groceries you provide in advance, perhaps when they pay the balance of their holiday.

Always make sure that left-over food from previous guests is removed from the property before new guests arrive. There is nothing worse then opening a cupboard and finding a half-empty bottle of ketchup with a dirty cap on view. Very few guests will use anything that has been left behind and you would be better to remove all traces of previous holiday-makers, even if this appears wasteful. In addition to the welcome tray, it is usually acceptable to leave condiments and herbs and spices for the use of all the guests, but replenish these as and when necessary if you do choose to provide them. Damp salt blocking the holes in the salt cellar and out-of-date herbs will not be accepted.

Pets allowed?

Deciding whether or not to allow pets into your property can be difficult. In general, I would advise you to 'ban' as little as possible, unless you have a valid reason for doing so. The location and type of property you have will have an affect on whether or not you allow pets to holiday with their owners. If you have a cottage in the middle of the countryside with scenic walks on your doorstep, you would be well advised to welcome dogs to your property. Most people holidaying in this kind of area will be walkers or, at the very least, lovers of the outdoors, and a high percentage of these people will own a dog. People who book holidays in this country and own pets do so because they can bring their pet along with them. Allowing pets into your property will, without a doubt, increase the number of bookings you receive if your property is in a rural position or near the seaside. Town and city centre flats are, of course, different and banning dogs from this kind of property may not have such a negative effect on your bookings.

The arguments for refusing to allow dogs are many and varied. Property owners worry about:

1. The smell the dogs may leave behind.
2. The hair the dogs may shed.
3. The damage to furniture and furnishings.

However, all these potential problems can be easily addressed by:

1. Ensuring the property is well aired upon departure: open windows to allow fresh air into the house.
2. Ensuring that carpets and furniture are vacuumed well.
3. Requesting that guests refrain from leaving their pets alone in the property and that they do not allow them on the furniture or in the bedrooms.

Many guests are very grateful for the chance to take their dogs on holiday with them and will nearly always agree to your terms.

My own experience has taught me that allowing guests to bring their pets is by far more advantageous with regard to running a successful holiday let business. The number of bookings I have received from guests with dogs has far outweighed the problems they have created. More than half of the guests who use my property bring their dogs with them. If, after weighing up the pros and cons, you still decide to ban dogs from your property, be prepared to rethink your decision if bookings are not forthcoming. If you are unsure of whether or not to allow dogs try restricting their number and size initially and see what, if any, damage is done. You could state that one small dog only will be allowed.

Often owners charge an additional amount for each pet, ranging from £10–£20, and I find that this charge more than covers the cost of any extra cleaning that may be required.

185

Smoking

This is another difficult decision, though for me it is not as hard as deciding whether to allow pets. This may be because I am a non-smoker who loves dogs! I personally do not allow smokers into my holiday property for a number of reasons:

1. The smell of smoke, unlike that of pets, is very difficult to eradicate, as it lingers for a long time.

2. Smoking is damaging to both paintwork (discolours white walls and ceilings) and furnishings (the smell gets into cushions and curtains and is difficult to get rid of).

3. You run a higher risk of potential fires due to unattended cigarettes or pipes.

4. You risk damaging carpets and furniture from cigarette burns.

5. You may alienate other holiday-makers who do not smoke and would not consider renting a property which allows smoking for the reasons listed above.

Banning smoking will reduce the number of potential guests to your property, so you must again weigh up the pros and cons before deciding whether or not to allow smoking. Nowadays far more people are aware of the damaging effects of smoking, and banning smokers from your property may not be too big an issue. If you decide to play it safe and refrain from banning smokers in your property, make sure smokers agree to certain terms:

1. Do not allow guests to smoke in the kitchen, bathrooms or bedrooms.

2. Ensure that guests are supplied with sufficient ashtrays.

3. Restrict the type of smoking to cigarettes and discourage cigars and pipes, which create heavier smells.

Children

It is not a good idea to ban children from your property, particularly in family-friendly areas such as at the seaside. You may get away with an 'adult only' property if you own a small one-bedroom flat or apartment in a city centre or a romantic cottage that appeals largely to couples, but a high percentage of people holidaying in self-catering properties in this country will be families. Often couples will opt for the luxury of a hotel, whereas families with two or more children prefer to book a self-catering property to allow them more freedom and because they are often much cheaper than booking a hotel.

Unless there are dangerous aspects to your property, such as a lake, railway track or steep/narrow staircases, I would advise you to resist the urge to ban children from your property. Wherever possible, make your property child-friendly and welcome families. The potential number of guests you will alienate by refusing children is immense and should be avoided at all costs. You may think that children will:

1. Run riot, be noisy and generally disrupt your neighbours.
2. Damage furniture and furnishings.
3. Smear chocolate and jam around the house.

However, in my own experience this is not usually the case. Most families on holiday will respect your property and will not allow their children any more freedom than they would encounter in their own homes. Of course there are exceptions to every rule, but then there is no guarantee if you ban smoking that your guests will heed this request.

Wherever possible, avoid putting any restrictions on your property, particularly in the first couple of years of renting it out. When you have built up a good database of holiday-makers who are regularly booking your property, you may be in a position to introduce some restrictions, should you feel it necessary. However, certainly for the first few years you should be looking to generate maximum rentals and this will be made all the more easy if you do not restrict yourself to childless couples who do not smoke or own a dog!

Complaints

It is to be hoped, if you follow the advice in this book, that you will not get customers who feel the need to complain. However, as with most things, you can never please all of the people all of the time. You *will* get people complaining from time to time. It is therefore important to know how to handle complaints and, most importantly, how to recognise a *genuine* complaint.

Genuine complaints

The number of genuine complaints should be relatively low if you take your time to prepare your holiday home to the highest standard and ensure that the facilities on offer are checked regularly. However, there may be some holiday-makers who have simply not enjoyed their holiday. Perhaps the weather was dreadful; if it rained constantly for a week they may have been cooped up in the house and had plenty of time to find fault. The weather, however, is out of your hands and you are not responsible for guests' enjoyment over and above the provision of the accommodation.

If you have invested in the services of a holiday let agency, you should have the added advice and protection they have to offer. It is highly likely that any disgruntled guests will contact your agency rather than you direct and put in their complaint – this is largely due to the fact that they have paid their money to the agency and received their correspondence from them. The agency will then contact you to notify you of the complaint and together you should be able to resolve the issue to everyone's satisfaction.

If, however, you have decided to 'go it alone' and have not put your property in the hands of an agent, you will need to know how to deal with irate customers. No property is exempt from criticism. A well-managed property in a sought-after location can still incur a problem.

You will need to know how to tell the difference between a serious complaint and one that is unjustified or exaggerated. If you are on hand to greet your guests on arrival, this is the best time to let them know how to contact you if a problem arises. It is important that you act quickly, should your guests have a complaint and, whenever possible, sort the problem out immediately. A guest who waits until the end of their stay to bring your attention to a faulty cooker will drastically reduce their credibility if they are intending to claim back expenses they have incurred having to eat at restaurants for the entire duration of their holiday.

If you are unable to greet your guests or visit them during their stay, then make sure that you display a contact name and telephone number clearly in the property, and make sure that your guests are aware that they can contact you at any time, should they feel the need.

If guests do complain you will inevitably feel disappointed. It can be very difficult to take criticism of your own property from a stranger, and guests can be quite rude if they do not feel they are getting value for money. Always remain calm and polite. Listen to the complaint first, without interrupting and before giving your own comments or reasons. If the problem can be rectified, make sure it is, immediately. If you feel the complaint is unjustified or exaggerated, politely explain this to the guests. Never take criticism personally and remember that your main aim is to resolve the issue as quickly as possible and ensure that your guests are happy. They may not return, and indeed you may not want them to. However, a happy customer is what you should always strive to achieve. Remember they may know dozens of potential customers and it is never a good idea to let holiday-makers leave unhappy if there is any way you can rectify things.

Compensation

You may be faced with a complaint that demands some kind of compensation. If you have enlisted the help of an agency, they should be in a good position to help you to decide whether or not a refund is necessary, and if so, the amount required. Rest assured that a decent agency will have seen a variety of incidents and will know exactly how to handle the situation.

If you are dealing with the complaint alone, you will need to decide whether or not there is any justification for the guest to demand a refund. The nature of the complaint, and how it has affected the holiday, will be the deciding factor in how much, if any, money you refund. Try to work out a solution with your guests. If they see that you are genuinely sorry about their complaint, and that you are attempting to make amends, the majority of people will be reasonable. Never feel tempted to refund the full amount of the cost of the holiday unless, of course, the property has been uninhabitable or dangerous. Remember that, if guests have remained at the property for the whole duration of their holiday, they will also have incurred costs such as gas, electricity, etc. and you should, at the very least, retain sufficient funds to cover these expenses.

CHAPTER 9 — INVENTORIES AND CHECK LISTS

Listing and checking contents

It is essential that you take the time to produce an inventory of all of the items in your property. This is not a job that can be done in half an hour and you would be wise to set aside a good few hours of your time to list all the items accurately.

An inventory will not be used by your guests but it will contain valuable information for you and your house-keeper. You may well walk into the living room of your property and know instantly if something has been moved or is missing, but your housekeeper will probably need several weeks on the job before she is as familiar with the property as you are. Providing her with a detailed list of items for each room will enable her to check things off quickly and easily, and notice at a glance if anything has been damaged, broken or stolen. In my experience, very few things are taken from holiday properties by the guests, not least because it would be easy for you to trace them at a later date. However, things will invariably get broken from time to time and, by having an inventory, you or your housekeeper will be able to see immediately if anything needs to be replaced.

It may not always be possible to check every item against the inventory after each changeover, as time will be of the essence, and the essential duties are to ensure the cleanliness of the property for the new guests. However, you or your housekeeper would be wise to make a thorough check of items against the inventory once a month. It is possible to overlook missing items and you may not notice that something has been broken for several weeks, so a thorough check periodically is necessary.

Most guests will inform you or your housekeeper if they have accidentally broken or damaged something, but a few may just hide the item or, worse still, throw it away and hope that you do not notice.

If you are marketing your property through an agent, they may well furnish you with an inventory for your kitchen. The kitchen is definitely the most time-consuming room of the house to compile an inventory for, and a pre-prepared list from an agent will be beneficial.

Although the initial compilation of the inventory will take time, you must also remember to update your list as and when you change or add to the contents of your property. Leave a copy of the inventory for your guests to peruse, should they so desire, furnish your housekeeper with another copy, and keep a third for your own reference. Instruct your housekeeper to make a check of the contents once a month and to inform you sooner if she notices that anything is broken or missing.

An inventory should look something like this:

Inventory – kitchen

Items required per person	No. supplied
Plates – large and small	
Mug	
Wine glass, tumbler	
Teacup and saucer	
Cutlery – knife, fork, soup spoon, dessert spoon, teaspoon	
Egg cup	

Kitchen equipment	No. supplied
Iron and ironing board	
Bread bin	
Biscuit and cake tins	
Breadboard/chopping boards	
Coffee maker/cafetiere	
Kettle	
Toaster/sandwich maker	
Measuring jug	
Casserole dish	
Pie dish	
Oven-to-table ware	
Teapot	
Baking tin/tray	
Butter dish	
Condiment set	
Wine rack	
Colander	
Frying pan	
Saucepans	
Water jug	
Knives – bread/carving/paring	
Scissors	
Bottle opener/cork screw	
Serving spoons	
Cooking utensils – ladle, fish slice, potato masher, etc.	
Wooden spoon	

Kitchen equipment	No. supplied
Tin opener	
Sieve	
Whisk	
Mop and bucket	
Tea towels, dishcloths and dusters	
Broom and dustpan and brush	
Washing line and pegs	
Tablecloths and table mats	
Ashtrays	
Dog feeding bowls and mats	
Torch	
Smoke alarms	
Fire extinguisher and fire blanket	
Oven gloves	

Your inventory for the kitchen will be the most comprehensive, as this room will contain many more items of equipment than any other in the house. Ask your housekeeper to make notes on her inventory of things she may need to inform you about. For example, if she thinks the tea towels are looking worn and need replacing or the saucepans have seen better days, these are the things she needs to be informing you of. You could ask her to post her completed inventory to you on a monthly basis, if you can't always get to visit the property yourself, so that you can see at a glance what you need to be stocking up on or replacing. Furnish your housekeeper with a new copy of the inventory on receipt of the completed one and update this as and when necessary.

The inventory for your bathroom may look like this:

Inventory – bathroom

Items provided	No. supplied
Bathroom scales	
Bath mat/pedestal mat	
Towels – bath and hand	
Cabinet	
Laundry basket	
Toilet roll holder	
Tumbler	
Mirror	

An inventory for the bedroom may include:

Inventory – bedroom

Items provided	No. supplied
Pictures	
Alarm clock	
Lamp	
Dressing table stool	
Dressing table mirror	
Coasters	
Cushions	
Ornaments	
Tissues/cotton wool/toiletries	
Bedspread/throw	

It is probably true to say that an inventory need only contain those items which are small, easy to break or can be easily removed from the property. It is not necessary to include items of furniture in the inventory unless you are intending to use your list to note down wear and tear, etc., so that you have a written record of everything in your property.

Inventories can be invaluable if you need to make a claim on your insurance in the event of a fire or flood. Owners of holiday properties have been known to experience thefts from their property by holiday-makers, and although this has never happened to me personally, if you do encounter this type of problem it is essential that you contact your letting agency immediately, as they are sure to have a policy in place for this type of problem. If you are letting the property yourself, depending on the nature of the object which you think has been stolen, you may prefer to put the situation down to experience and make a note not to allow those particular guests to re-book with you. If you are intending to contact the guests, be very careful how you tackle them. It is important to remember that:

1. They may well have had an accident and broken the object. It would be terrible if you contacted them with all guns blazing and accused them of stealing something when they had genuinely broken the item. They may have intended to inform you and simply forgotten.

2. The missing object may have been moved to avoid breakage. For example, guests with a lively dog or small child may move an ornament out of harm's way and forget to replace it when they leave. Before contacting anyone over an item you consider is missing, make sure you have a good look all over the house first.

3. The object may have been missing for several weeks and could have been broken by guests holidaying in the property previously. Do not assume that the last guests in are the ones to blame, unless you are certain that you have methodically checked your inventory after *every* guest has left.

Breakages

This is rather a difficult matter to address. On the whole, my own experience has taught me that few holiday-makers will abuse your accommodation, and that if any breakages occur they are usually accidental rather than malicious. Anyone can have an accident and, with this in mind, it seems rather unfair to expect guests to pay for replacements. After all, running a holiday let business will incur costs from time to time, and this is something you should expect and be willing to cover the losses yourself. That said, some holiday let owners insist on guests paying for damage to their property, whether this is intentional or accidental.

Recouping costs for damages

There are a number of ways you can recoup money for damage or breakages, and you may like to consider the following:

1. Ask your guests to pay a small deposit or bond, refundable at the end of their stay. Bear in mind though that this additional request for money may alienate potential guests and limit your bookings. Insisting that guests pay a bond also conjures up thoughts of past holiday-makers. Potential guests may well consider your property attracts the wrong kind of holiday-maker and this can be very off-putting.

2. You may like to leave a note in the information folder setting out your policy for breakages. Some owners request that guests leave a note informing them of any breakages and ask that they either replace the broken item themselves or leave sufficient money to cover the cost of a replacement. Bear in mind that not everyone will read your information folder, and those that do may ignore your request.

Broken wine glasses, cups and plates are par for the course in everyday life, and guests holidaying in your property will not be immune to this kind of accidental damage. I would recommend that you seriously consider the implications of trying to recoup your losses for small items of everyday equipment. Chasing up guests, confronting them and finally extracting money from them all seems like a lot of hassle for a £3 wine glass. The trick here is to make sure that you equip your property with standard, reasonably priced equipment, particularly with regard to everyday items, and refrain from trying to impress with cut-glass crystal champagne flutes; that way any breakages can be easily replaced without breaking the bank.

Any major damage to your property that appears to be non-accidental must be dealt with appropriately. Depending on the nature of the damage, you may like to consider making a claim on your property's household insurance.

CHAPTER 10
THE FINANCIAL ASPECT

Council tax

The amount of council tax you will be required to pay on your holiday let property will depend very much on the area your property is in and the authority it is under. In some areas, owners of second properties are allowed the luxury of a 50 per cent reduction in council tax, while others are required to pay 90 per cent of the full cost.

Whatever the charge, you will need to make sure that you have sufficient funds to pay this tax. You will be required to pay council tax every month, regardless of whether your property is being let or not.

At the time of writing, if your investment property is available for holiday letting for 19 weeks or fewer per annum, you will be required to pay council tax. If it is available for letting for 20 weeks or more per annum, you will be required to pay business rates.

If your property is in an area where council tax on second homes is high, or has recently been increased, you will probably benefit from paying business rates as these often work out cheaper, and in some cases councils are granting 50 per cent small business relief. In order to qualify for business rates your property *must* be available to rent for a minimum of 20 weeks per annum, otherwise you will fail the Inland Revenue's tests and will not be eligible to be treated as a business and thereby lose out on a huge amount of valuable tax breaks.

Value added tax

The threshold for VAT is currently £60,000. If you have several properties available for letting, you may well breach this threshold. However, if you are only intending to buy and let one property, it is highly unlikely that you will exceed the £60,000 limit.

It is vital that you seek the advice of an accountant if you are in any doubt whatsoever about the implications of VAT on your property.

Capital gains tax

When you sell a property, which is not your family home or principal private residence, then in general you will be liable to pay capital gains tax on it. However, nothing is ever simple when it comes to taxation and the situation can change from one year to the next and each individual person's tax position can be very different. You would be well advised to seek the advice of an accountant for clarification of your own personal position and liabilities.

Although at the present time, capital gains tax is payable on investment property which is not your principal private residence, there are still ways of reducing your liability. It is vital that you ensure that you enjoy your annual exemption limit, which doubles for a married couple, if the property is in joint names. Unmarried couples can choose a main residence each and benefit from the annual allowance this way. You may be eligible for additional relief if the investment property has ever been used as your main residence.

Inheritance tax

Properties that are used solely for holiday letting will probably qualify as business assets with regard to inheritance tax. At present (2006/7), inheritance tax is charged at 40 per cent on the amount of the estate valued over £285,000; however, if the property qualifies for exclusion through being a business asset, then the relief is 100%. Although it is not a guarantee that all holiday letting properties are excluded from business asset relief, the Inland Revenue

Advanced Practice Manual suggests that where a property qualifies as a business, relief *should* be granted.

Taxable profit

If you own a property in the United Kingdom which you let out, you can deduct certain expenses and tax allowances from your rental income in order to work out your taxable profit, or indeed loss. If you own several letting properties, you can pool the income and expenses together.

If your property keeps to the 'rules' listed below, which are known as 'qualifying tests', then the rental income you receive from your holiday home in the United Kingdom may be treated differently, for the purposes of tax, to other rental income.

In order for your property to qualify as a 'holiday let', it must:

1. Be in the United Kingdom.
2. Be fully furnished.
3. Be available for holiday letting to the public for a minimum of 140 days per annum.
4. Be actually let as a holiday home for at least 70 days per annum. To qualify these lets *must* be commercial lets and not rented at cheap rates for friends or family.
5. Be let on a short-term basis of not more than 31 consecutive days. You will not be able to let the property to the same person for more than 31 days per annum.
6. Be let as a holiday home for a period of at least seven months per annum.

It is worth knowing that if you meet all the above qualifying tests in a seven-month period of each year, there are no restrictions on longer lets for the remaining five-month period. You will be able to let your property for whatever length of time you wish in the remainder of the year. However, you must be aware that these lets, if over 31 days, will not count as holiday lets.

Allowable expenses

When owning a holiday let property it is vital that you are aware of the numerous expense allowances you will be able to claim against tax.

Generally, it is true to say that if the expenditure is wholly or exclusively for the purpose of the holiday let business, it is likely to be an allowable expense for tax purposes. Holiday letting demands a good deal of management and therefore a realistic amount for wages can be claimed.

The usual allowable expenses for a holiday let property are as follows:

Accountancy Charges	Fees incurred for the preparation of accounts. This does not include the fee paid for the preparation of tax returns.
Advertising and Marketing	Commission paid to an agent, together with any other marketing costs such as newspaper advertisements, etc.
Rent/Rates/Insurance	Council tax, business rates, insurance, water rates, etc.
Interest and Finance	Interest on loans for the purpose of acquiring or improving the property for

	let, together with arrangement fees and interest on hire purchase agreements to buy furniture, etc.
Heat and Light	Gas, electricity and fuel specifically relating to the property, or a proportion of the same if the property is attached to the owner's personal residence.
Printing, Postage and Stationery	The cost of stamps, paper, printing leaflets, brochures, etc. in relation to the holiday let property.
Repairs and Maintenance	Painting, decorating and general maintenance.
Services	The services you provide for the upkeep of the property, including caretaker, gardener and cleaner. Make sure you are aware of any PAYE implications.
Garden	Expenses incurred maintaining or improving the garden of the property, including plants, etc.
Crockery, Cutlery and Linen	These items will need replacing often due to breakages and wear and tear. Items such as bed linen, towels, pillows, cutlery, plates, dishes, etc. are allowable expenses.

Telephone	Telephone calls made in relation to the holiday let property.
Cleaning Materials and Consumables	Washing-up liquid, dishcloths, floor cloths, bin liners, toilet rolls, soap, light bulbs, etc.
Motor Vehicle Expenses	You will be allowed an annual mileage rate on journeys to and from the holiday let property, providing it is for business purposes and not private visits. Other journeys, which are for the sole purpose of acquiring supplies for the property, can also be claimed.
Sundry Expenses	Costs incurred for the provision of welcome packs, flowers, toiletries, refuse collections, window cleaning, television licence, etc.

Capital allowances

Capital allowances cover the depreciation of furnishings and other assets purchased, excluding vehicles. Kitchen and bathroom fittings and heating systems are included in any capital allowance.

Capital expenditure on certain items also qualifies for capital allowances. These items include:

White goods and electrical equipment

Furniture

Carpets and floor coverings

Ornaments

Pictures

Garden furniture and equipment

In addition to the above, expenditure on the following also qualifies for capital allowances:

The installation of fitted kitchens

The installation of fitted bathrooms

Central heating

Forty per cent of the cost of these assets can be claimed in the first year only, with normal capital allowances of 25 per cent for second and subsequent years. For example:

A heating system (purchased September 2005)	£5,000
First year allowance @ 40 per cent	(£2,000)
Balance carried forward	£3,000
Second and subsequent years	
Balance brought forward	£3,000
Allowance against income @ 25 per cent	£750

It is extremely important that you are aware of the capital allowances you can claim against your holiday letting income. The availability of this allowance can make it possible to turn a profit – on which you will pay tax – to a loss – on which tax refunds may be available.

Working out your taxable profit or loss

The profit or loss you make on your holiday let property is worked out in much the same way as any other rental income. However, on a holiday let property you will be able to claim capital allowances rather than the usual wear and tear allowance. The previous list gives examples of expenses which will qualify for capital allowances.

There are certain financial records you will need to keep relating to your holiday let business. These records should include:

1. The amount of rental income you have received during the year.
2. A list of your allowable expenses.
3. Details of your capital costs.

Rental Income You will need to keep a written record of the dates you have let your property and the rents you have charged.

Allowable Expenses You will need to keep a written record detailing all the costs you have incurred in letting and managing your rental property. The allowable expenses you claim will reduce the amount of taxable profit you make. A detailed list of allowable expenses is given earlier in this chapter and they will include things such as buildings and contents insurance, maintenance and repair costs, utility bills, council tax, agency letting fees, etc.

Capital Costs You will be able to reduce your taxable profit by claiming certain allowances for 'capital costs'. These include the cost of the furniture and equipment you provide in your property.

If you employ an agency to let your property, you will receive a detailed statement of the rental income you have made. You should keep all of these statements, together with a log of your allowable and capital expenses showing which items you have purchased, when you purchased them and how much you paid. Keep all your receipts.

If you are letting the property yourself, you must be extra vigilant when it comes to recording the rental income you have received. Make sure you keep a rent book showing the dates your property is let and the income you have received. Again, ensure you keep all receipts and invoices and keep your business expenses separate from your personal expenses.

You will need to declare the money you make from your furnished holiday property. You can do this by completing the land and property pages of your Self Assessment tax return. If you own more than one letting property in the United Kingdom, and your total income from all the properties is under £15,000 per annum before expenses, then you can group the expenses together as a single total on your tax return. If the amount is over £15,000 you will be required to provide separate detailed information for each property along with a full tax return.

You will need to keep all your property let records for six years after the tax year in which they apply.

Profit or loss?

A crucial difference between holiday letting and long-term letting is shown clearly with regard to profit and loss on the business. If a holiday let business is operated as a husband and wife partnership, you will be able to maximise your tax liabilities by allocating profits to the lowest earner. In much the same way, if a loss is incurred this can be allocated to the highest earner's income, which will in turn maximise the tax refunds available.

In the case of a holiday let, losses can be offset against other income to obtain tax refunds or they can be carried forward to use against future profits. If a loss is incurred in the first four years of a holiday let business, you would be able to carry the loss back three years. For example, a loss suffered in the year to 5 April 2005 could be offset against the income earned in 2001/2002. This could be a crucial benefit if the earnings were higher in the earlier years.

Another advantage of holiday letting is that where profits are earned, tax liabilities can be reduced (and future pension benefits increased) by the facility to increase pension premiums because the profit is treated as income for pension purposes.

While it is important to be aware of the numerous benefits available for a holiday let business, it must also be remembered that you should be setting up your business with a view to making a profit. If your business does not succeed, at some point, in making a profit, it will fail to meet the tests enabling it to be treated favourably for tax purposes. For this reason it is important that you consider, from the outset, what your aims are, and that you prepare a brief business plan to support your business should there be any queries on this matter by the Inland Revenue.

USEFUL ADDRESSES
AND WEBSITES

DHC ACCOUNTING LIMITED
Unit 7 Lillyhall Business Centre
Jubilee Road
Workington
Cumbria
CA14 4HA
Telephone 01900 64464

HOLIDAY COTTAGES GROUP LIMITED
Incorporating Country Holidays
Welcome Cottages and Blake's Cottages
Spring Mill
Earby
Barnoldswick
Lancashire
BB94 0AA
Telephone 01282 844284
www.cendantvrg.co.uk

RECOMMENDED COTTAGE HOLIDAYS LTD
Eastgate House
Pickering
North Yorkshire
YO18 7DW
Telephone 08700 718718
www.recommended-cottages.co.uk

ENGLISH TOURISM COUNCIL
Fulfilment Centre
Thames Tower
Black's Road
Hammersmith
London
W6 9EL
Telephone 0208 8469000
www.visitbritain.com
A copy of the 'Pink Booklet' giving details of various regulations with regard to holiday let properties can be obtained from the English Tourism Council.

S.S.C. ROTALUX LTD
The Old Stables
38a Cemetery Road
Southport
PR8 6RD
Telephone 01704 500386
www.hotel-toiletries.com

THE STATIONERY OFFICE PUBLICATIONS CENTRE
PO Box 276
London
SW8 5DT
Contact them for a copy of The Furniture and Furnishings
(Fire) (Safety) Regulations.

INDEX

If you want to know how … to do your own book-keeping and accounting

'In "doing the books" you will be at the very heart of the business, with your hands on the controls. You will be involved in the management of its assets and liabilities, its expenses and its profit margins.'

Peter Taylor

Book-keeping & Accounting for the Small Business
How to keep the books and maintain financial control over your business
Peter Taylor

'A guide to accounting procedures for sole traders, partnerships and limited companies… includes real life examples' – *The Times*

'Compulsory reading for those starting a new business and for those already in the early stages.' – *Manager, National Westminster Bank (Midlands)*

'An easy-to-understand manual on double-entry book-keeping that anyone can follow.' – *Business First*

ISBN   1 85703 878 9

If you want to know how ... to keep your home and your family safe from crime

"There is a lot that the average person can do to protect themselves, their family and their property. This book will teach you how to perform a security review on your home and show you what countermeasures you can take to ensure that you are *highly unlikely* to be a victim of crime."

Des Conway

The Home Security Handbook
How to keep your home and family safe from crime

D. G. Conway

Surveys have revealed that when asked what people worry most about for themselves and their family 45% of them said 'CRIME'. Crime statistics certainly indicate that people have good reason to worry: A burglary takes place on average every 30 seconds in the UK.

Alarming though this and other statistics may be, this book will show you how you can use them to reduce the risk of becoming a crime statistic yourself. It will teach you how to audit and review your home and lifestyle, to identify a range of vulnerabilities, threats and risks and then show you how to provide effective countermeasures to avoid the threat and reduce the risk.

The countermeasures suggested are designed to be realistic, achievable at minimal cost and effort and simple enough to be introduced or implemented by the average person.

Des Conway has over 20 years security experience, which combines police service with commercial security consultancy. He has experienced countless security reviews of domestic and commercial properties, delivering reports highlighting vulnerabilities, and recommending simple, affordable and achievable countermeasures.

ISBN 1 84528 024 5

If you want to know how … to be a property millionaire

TV star Annie Hulley has amassed a substantial property portfolio in just three years. In this book she explains how she achieved it, the mistakes she made along the way, and what she's gleaned from the experience.

'I now have a substantial investment property portfolio and that is the reason for writing this book, to show that from humble beginnings you too can achieve your goal of being a property millionaire.'

Annie Hulley

How to be a Property Millionaire
From Coronation Street to Canary Wharf
Annie Hulley

'A must-read book…a practical guide for anyone who has an interest in investing in bricks and mortar.' – *OPP*

'…loads of advice on getting on the property ladder in the UK, plus a section on holiday lets and second homes … and a chapter with advice on buying in foreign markets.' – *Homes Worldwide*

'Hulley's guide covers a huge range of subjects relating to buying property, including different types of mortgages, buying at auctions, buying off plan, tax liabilities, estate agents, holiday homes and much more. She's done her homework.' – *Observer*

ISBN 1 85703 857 6

If you want to know how ... to invest in the stock market

This book explains in plain English all there is to know about what affects share prices, how to avoid unnecessary risks and how to trade on the stock market, whether it's up or down.

Investing in Stocks & Shares
A step-by-step guide to making money on the stock market
Dr John White

'Will be a help to private investors...Gives an easy-to-understand guide to the way the stock market works, and how the investor should go about setting up a suitable investment strategy.' – *What Investment*

'If you have got money to spare, start by investing in the purchase of this book.' – *Making Money*

'User-friendly... Contains practical examples and illustrations of typical share-dealing documents...demystifies the world of stocks and shares.' – *OwnBase*

ISBN   1 85703 847 9

If you want to know how ... to start and run your own business

'Running your own business can be a very rewarding and fulfilling experience, but there are no secret tricks to being successful... Success will only come through hard work and through always offering something that the consumer wants, at the right price, in the right place, and in the right quantity. This book covers all the essential points you need to know and think about before you actually go ahead and start your own business.'

Alan Le Marinel

Start and Run Your Own Business
The complete guide to setting up and managing a small business
Alan Le Marinel

Whether you dream of owning a corner shop or starting the next High Street chain, there are few more exciting prospects than starting your own business. This book will guide you through the whole start up process and steer you on towards success. It will help with:

✓ Defining your business strategy
✓ Researching the market and setting the right price
✓ Writing a business plan and raising finance
✓ Recruiting and managing staff
✓ Forecasting, budgeting and accounting
✓ Buying an existing business or franchise

Recommended by the Sunday Times – Business

ISBN 1 85703 988 2

If you want to know how ... to make your first property purchase a success

'The sense of achievement gained from buying a first property is tremendous. It is a momentous occasion, filled with pride and contentment.

'It is true that there is a growing trend and an ever expanding ability to buy property, but there is associated with it a mountainous capacity for critical mistakes. This book is intended for savvy investors who wish to evade such errors. By following the advice laid out in this book, conducting a thorough personal assessment, investigating properties worthy of purchase and exploring all the alternatives, you will find yourself able to buy a dwelling that meets your needs and one that provides financial security for the future.'

Tony Booth

The Beginner's Guide to Property Investment
The ultimate handbook for first-time buyers and would-be property investors
Tony Booth

This book provides an insight into many key issues; it explains what constitutes a sound investment, how you can examine your borrowing potential and create a golden credit rating, what mortgages are available and which are most suitable. It also discusses alternative property investment; buy-to-let, let-to-buy, renovation, buying property abroad, self-build and self-employed business enterprise; and shares generous amounts of inside information and well-kept trade secrets.

ISBN 1 85703 961 0

If you want to know how ... to start your own business

'The road you live in, the bakery you stop at to get your morning coffee and pastry, the pub you frequent; none of it would be there if someone hadn't dreamed about it first. This workbook aims to help you shape your dreams of running your own business into rock-solid reality, acting as a guide for each step of the way.'

Cheryl D. Rickman

The Small Business Start-up Workbook
A step-by-step guide to starting the business you've dreamed of
Cheryl D. Rickman

An up-to-date approach to self-employment and business start-up, this workbook shows you how to research your business idea, plan the right marketing strategies and manage effective teams. It offers a selection of:

✓ real-life case studies
✓ practical exercises
✓ checklists
✓ worksheets

Other well-known entrepreneurs reveal what they would have done differently, what their biggest mistakes have been and what they've learnt: Dame Anita Roddick, Julie Meyer, Stelios Haji-Ioannou, Simon Woodroffe and others expose their best and worst decisions and contribute their tips for succeeding in business.

ISBN 1 84528 038 5

How To Books are available through all good bookshops, or you can order direct from us through Grantham Book Services.

Tel: +44 (0)1476 541080
Fax: +44 (0)1476 541061
Email: orders@gbs.tbs-ltd.co.uk

Or via our website

www.howtobooks.co.uk

To order via any of these methods please quote the title(s) of the book(s) and your credit card number together with its expiry date.

For further information about our books and catalogue, please contact:

How To Books
Spring Hill House
Spring Hill Road
Begbroke
Oxford OX5 1RX

Visit our web site at

www.howtobooks.co.uk

Or you can contact us by email at info@howtobooks.co.uk